DEDICATION

In memory of my parents

Thomas Sedley Bridgewater
6th July 1913 — 25th September 1973

&

Elsie Margaret Bridgewater
4th February 1920 — 1st June 1985

&

John & Alan, my brothers in arms

D1388677

OTHER TITLES IN THIS SERIES:-

The Art of Mindful Baking

The Art of Mindful Birdwatching

The Art of Mindful Gardening

The Art of Mindful Silence

The Art of Mindful Singing

The Art of Mindful Walking

Einstein and the Art of Mindful Cycling

Galileo and the Art of Ageing Mindfully

Happiness and How it Happens

The Heart of Mindful Relationships

The Joy of Mindful Writing

The Mindful Art of Wild Swimming

Mindful Crafting

The Mindful Man

Mindful Pregnancy and Birth

Mindful Travelling

Mindfulness and Compassion

Mindfulness and Music

Mindfulness and Surfing

Mindfulness and the Art of Drawing

Mindfulness and the Art of Managing Anger

Mindfulness and the Art of Urban Living

Mindfulness and the Natural World

Mindfulness at Work

Mindfulness for Black Dogs and Blue Days

Mindfulness for Students

Mindfulness for Unravelling Anxiety

The Mindfulness in Knitting

The Practice of Mindful Yoga

Zen and the Path of Mindful Parenting

Mindfulness *and the* Journey *of* Bereavement

Restoring Hope After Death

Peter Bridgewater

Leaping Hare Press

This paperback edition published in the UK in 2019 by
Leaping Hare Press
An imprint of The Quarto Group
The Old Brewery, 6 Blundell Street
London N7 9BH, United Kingdom
T (0)20 7700 6700 F (0)20 7700 8066
www.QuartoKnows.com

First published in hardback in 2015

Text copyright © 2014 Peter Bridgewater
Design and layout copyright © 2017 Quarto Publishing plc

British Library Cataloguing-in-Publication Data
A catalogue record for this book is available from the British Library

ISBN: 978-1-78240-933-5

This book was conceived, designed and produced by
Leaping Hare Press
58 West Street, Brighton BN1 2RA, United Kingdom

Creative Director PETER BRIDGEWATER
Publisher SUSAN KELLEY
Commissioning Editor MONICA PERDONI
Editorial Director TOM KITCH
Senior Project Editor CAROLINE EARLE
Editor JENNI DAVIS
Designer GINNY ZEAL
Illustrator MELVYN EVANS

Printed in China

1 3 5 7 9 10 8 6 4 2

CONTENTS

Foreword 06

INTRODUCTION
The Sound of Bereavement 08

CHAPTER ONE
Denial 38

CHAPTER TWO
Anger 58

CHAPTER THREE
Bargaining 78

CHAPTER FOUR
Depression 98

CHAPTER FIVE
Acceptance 114

An Afterword 134

Endnotes 140

Index 142

FOREWORD

◆

Mindfulness and the Journey of Bereavement is a wonderful book. Peter Bridgewater has accomplished a remarkable outcome by combining his experience, insight and wisdom. As a bereavement volunteer, he knows what it feels like when one is drowning in a sea of sorrow after the death of a dear relative or a beloved friend.

Peter narrates a number of moving stories full of humanity, vulnerability and tenderness. I was deeply touched by the emotions and experiences of people who have gone through the dark night of desperation, grief, guilt, fear, anger, blame, isolation and separation, but who with counselling and mindful support, have come out of that darkness into the light of understanding and relief.

Peter is in a unique position to work with the bereaved and to write this book. He has gone through profound pain himself. Both his parents died through suicide and I can well imagine the wounds and scars inflicted on the loved ones left behind. But, with the remedy of time and awareness, Peter was able to focus not on what his parents took away, but on what they gave him. This is the miracle of mindfulness, which acted as a rescue remedy for the soul.

Elisabeth Kübler-Ross has been the greatest inspiration to Peter in writing this book. Kübler-Ross no doubt was an exceptional woman, able to understand, appreciate and explore the universal meaning of death. Her five stages of grief – Denial, Anger, Bargaining, Depression and Acceptance – are essential touchstones on the journey to peaceful reconciliation with the fact and phenomenon of loss and suffering due to death. The visionary hypothesis of Kübler-Ross combined with the practical advice and guidance of Peter Bridgewater makes this book an outstanding companion to all those who are in need of help and support at traumatic times.

Peter has included some beautiful and enlightening quotes from The Buddha to Carl Jung. Reading these words alongside the rest of the book, one arrives at a deeper understanding of loss. Ultimately we realize that one need not fear one's own death or that of others. After all, death is not the end of life, it is a door into new life, as life is eternal. The Bhagavad Gita, the sacred text of the Hindus, says that as we discard old clothes in favour of new, we discard our old body in favour of a new body. So death is welcome as a liberating force. We rejoice at the time of birth but there can be no birth without death. Therefore we should also celebrate death as the accomplishment of life's journey. In our mindful meditation we can reach a state of equanimity and acceptance. This is the profound meaning of this book.

SATISH KUMAR
✝ *Peace & environmental activist*
✝ *Founder of* Resurgence *magazine*
✝ *Co-founder of Schumacher College*

THE SOUND OF BEREAVEMENT

*My first bereavement was the suicide of my
father. I was twenty-one, about to leave art school,
my whole life ahead. His death created a tsunami
of grief that overwhelmed but didn't quite swallow me
up. I felt insecure and angry throughout my twenties,
furious towards both of my parents for their
psychological legacy, deaf to my needs. I buried myself
deeply in work and hedonism, blocking out the noise,
not hearing my emotional discord. Listening to the
melody now, reflecting, writing about loss four decades
later, my father's death chimes gently and more
harmoniously in the composition
of my life.*

LIFE & DEATH

◆

*Birth and death are the inescapable, universal truths of human exist-
ence. The death of somebody close, whom we love, is earth-shattering.
It can literally tear our world apart, filling us with feelings of longing, sadness, loneliness, fear, guilt – even hopelessness and despair.*

THE SHOCK AND PAIN OF LOSING SOMEONE central to our
life is overwhelming. There might be physical symptoms
of grief such as fatigue, a hollow feeling in the pit of the stomach, tightness across the throat and chest, disturbed sleep
patterns, social withdrawal, absent-mindedness and crying.
We may feel numb and completely lost – or so distressed,
angry and emotionally volatile that we just can't see the point
in going on. Our feelings of despair might be so great that we
question the very purpose of existence and ask ourselves
'what is there left to live for?'.[1]

Grief is the natural response to loss. We grieve when parted
from any deep attachment. It might be the loss of country,
job, spouse (through divorce), a family pet or a friend; but the
most debilitating form of grief comes with the death of a
much-loved person. Death shakes our world. Although
bereavement is universal and something that we all come face
to face with during our lives, each experience of grief is
exclusive. The sounds of bereavement are personal requiems;
we each hear death's haunting melodies differently.

A Feeling of Madness

There is no normal or right way to grieve, and no time frame, so it is best to express our grief in any way that feels natural. How we react to loss will be influenced by many things: age, personality, cultural background, spiritual beliefs; our personal circumstances; how we cope with trauma; our previous experience of loss and our social networks. Every person and relationship is unique, and so is each experience of death.

Grief, when it hits, can seem like madness. We feel every blow. It punches the stomach and beats the mind. It can knock

---

◆

"'The pain of grief is just as much a part of life
as the joy of love; it is, perhaps, the price we pay for love,
the cost of commitment." (Parkes, Colin Murray, 1987).
The resolution of grief can be accomplished by developing
mindfulness. The practice of mindfulness (also called satipatthana:
sati meaning *awareness* and patthana meaning *keeping present*),
emphasizes being aware and surrendering to the natural
and present moment conditions of mind and body. This is
primarily a Theravadin Buddhist approach. However, elements
of its practice can be found within common task oriented and
supportive grief counselling techniques, as well as
some modern psychotherapies.'

FROM 'GRIEF AND THE MINDFULNESS APPROACH'
MALCOLM HUXTER [2]

◆

us down. The emotional pain of loss can be so intensely powerful that the manifestations are mortifying: we feel frightened and anxious; we might hear the voice of our loved one, find ourselves talking aloud to them in the street or see them sitting there in front of us; we might smell their scent or feel certain that soon they will be coming home – that they are not really dead after all; we might be privately relieved that death has arrived and the suffering is over – theirs and ours. We may also feel so exhausted and in such turmoil that we just want to go to sleep and never wake up. None of these feelings are unnatural or wrong – they are normal reactions to what might well be the most difficult time of our life.

INTRODUCING MINDFULNESS

We all have to endure death during the course of our lives and we each have to travel the protracted and arduous road of bereavement. It can be a traumatic and isolating trek. This book teaches us to use the transformative practice of mindfulness to support us constructively on our formidable journey.

BY ENGAGING FULLY IN THE PRESENT MOMENT – by being mindful – we can calm our troubled minds and accept the experience of bereavement in a wiser and, long term, more positive way. Life can never, and will never, be the same for us following the death of someone we love but, hopefully,

'There is no need to go to India or anywhere else to find peace. You will find that deep place of silence right in your room, your garden or even your bathtub.'

ELISABETH KÜBLER-ROSS (1926–2004)
PSYCHIATRIST & AUTHOR

there will eventually come a time when we will be able to adjust to life without that person and begin looking towards the future. We may experience their absence so fiercely that we feel unable to face what lies ahead without them – but there is a way through this dark maze of despair and, given time, those feelings usually change.

As we travel through grief we should gradually begin to accept the physical loss of our loved one and hold the relationship to us in a new perspective. Life goes on – it really does. There will always be a gap, sorrow and someone central missing from our life but there are still many wonderful experiences and things worth living for, although it takes time to recognize this and recover.

The Anchor of Mindfulness
Mindfulness is about noticing our thoughts in a way that allows us to observe the inner landscape of our lives: our thoughts; our physical sensations; our feelings. It is a form of mental training and awareness that enables us to concentrate

on the here-and-now and live more authentically in the moment. It is a way of paying attention to ourselves and to the world around us, of waking up our senses and relaxing into our present experience of NOW, however good, bad or indifferent the present happens to be.

For most of us most of the time, our minds are spinning with thoughts, we are too easily distracted and therefore absent to much of our physical experience. We live in our heads more than the moment. Instead, our emphasis *Seize* should be on the present moment: on reality. *the day.* The past is a foreign country[3] to which we can never return. It endures only in memory. The future is another flight of fancy – not yet here. Tomorrow exists only in our imagination.

We are constantly striving to reach goals: worrying about the future, ruminating about the past and struggling to cope with the pressure of busy lives. Mindfulness is the tool that allows us to anchor ourselves firmly into the present moment and wholly appreciate whatever we are experiencing: the glorious colour of an autumn day; the sound of the sea; the warmth of the sun on our body; the thirst-quenching juice of a peach; a good conversation. The wonderment of life, pleasure as well as pain, is there for us to delight in. The simple, complete enjoyment of the present second – not past, nor future – is difficult to sustain but the present moment is the only experience guaranteed. *Seize the day.*[4]

Reasons to be Mindful

Mindfulness is based on the Buddhist practice of recognizing and accepting the reality of the present and of living in it fully. It is choosing to notice the smallest details of our experiences, in the moment, and relishing them. It is about clearing our whirling minds enough to understand ourselves better and, in so doing, make the small adjustments necessary to help us embrace harsh realities in life, such as bereavement, that we cannot alter. The death of somebody we love brings enormous turbulence into our lives; day-to-day routines are turned upside down, as well as hopes and plans for the future. Our sense of separation feels like we are being cut in two and part of us is lost forever. Mindfulness can help us heal by grounding us firmly in the present.

Mindfulness is a positive way of concentrating our mind, regulating our breath and harnessing our thoughts. It is an effective meditation tool to stop our thoughts from rambling, in order to acknowledge them and find quietude and peace. Mindfulness can change the way we think about ourselves. Instead of attacking ourselves for being bad, impatient, morose, overreactive, indecisive – whatever – daily practice helps us manage our moods and re-evaluate our opinion of ourselves, thereby increasing self-esteem and reducing self-doubt. Available to everyone, whether religious or secular, mindfulness can soothe us during the fraught journey through grief and benefit our lives greatly going forwards.

The Buddha & The Baby

Two thousand five hundred years ago, The Buddha used a performance-based technique to help a bereaved woman accept the reality of her child's death. The woman's child died not long after it could walk, and in a distressed state, the woman wandered the streets for days with the child in her arms, asking everyone for a medicine to save her child. The Buddha, seeing her behaviour, told her that he knew of a medicine to help her but first she had to collect a handful of mustard seeds, each one from a house that had not seen death. As she went from house to house, unable to collect the seeds, she realized that death in general, and the death of her child in particular, was a reality. Through insight she discarded her irrational behaviour.[5]

Mindfulness calms our minds, regenerates our spirits and relieves stress. It helps us regain control over the high levels of anxiety and depression that overwhelm us when somebody we love dies. Mindful practice helps push away the repetitive wheel of gloom that rolls over and crushes us during grieving. Bringing mindfulness into our life doesn't mean we have to become a Buddhist monk, or sit cross-legged on the floor, nor chant mantras. Learning how to be mindful simply offers alternative ways of responding to suffering and the hard realities we have to face at such agonizing times.

HOW CAN WE FEEL BETTER?

◆

Everyday life is an endless cycle of interrelating emotions. Joy and sorrow: laughter and tears. We should cling to neither and embrace both. Mindfulness invites us to see a situation clearly and, in so doing, choose how we respond, rather than being prisoner to pre-conditioned reactions, which make us feel worse.

WE CAN ALL LEARN TO BE IN THE MOMENT through our senses. After all, it is only possible to fully appreciate a warm, sunny day because we know the feeling of a damp, cold one. Fortunately, being human is not limited to one fixed state or condition. Existence is a journey full of amazing contradictions. Life reveals itself to be an astonishing blend of joy and sadness, hot and cold, night and day, ying and yang. These conditions are not separate, opposing forces but complementary and interdependent sensations. Nothing is rigid, permanent or continuous in life. Each day is born and then dies.

Life is never the same after the death of somebody we love but then life is never the same from one day to the next. Practising mindfulness soothes our depression or anxiety and teaches us to recognize that it is fruitless pushing against, struggling with, or clinging on to things we want but cannot have.[6] Mindfulness is the complete enjoyment of the fleeting moment that brings with it a truly authentic experience of what it means to be utterly alive.

Feel the Breath

Mindfulness is about waking up, connecting with ourselves and the world around and appreciating the experience of now. This art of conscious living can profoundly increase our satisfaction in the small, everyday events that constitute our lives. Mindfulness brings complete attention to our present experience, moment by moment, here and now, helping relieve our feelings of loss and detachment.

Our breath: always with us, essential to existence and yet, often unnoticed. Breathing is the most basic yet fundamental experience of life. If our breath ceased we would cease. Becoming aware of our breath enriches our participation in everything we do. Try it now. Close your eyes and bring your attention to your body, to the movement of your breath, the expansion in your rib cage. Focusing on our breathing allows us to feel more vital: taking in, giving out; relaxing, letting go; the in-breath; the out-breath.[7]

Bringing our attention to this most basic yet essential ingredient of life – our breath – will help us reflect on the true nature of loss. It will help us cope. Mindful practice increases self-awareness and reduces disturbed, reactive

◆

'Should you shield the valleys from the windstorms,

you would never see the beauty of their canyons.'

ELISABETH KÜBLER-ROSS

◆

feelings towards the experience of grief. By feeling more connected to the world, and to ourselves, we feel less erratic emotionally. Paying attention to the present moment brings more stability, calm and peacefulness into our lives. Mindfulness helps us to breathe, be calm, more in tune with our emotions and face what we cannot avoid.

The Kiss of Life

Engagement with breathing and appreciating every breath we take refreshes our wonderment at living in the moment. It will shake us out from our slumbers. Yes, we know we are alive: our dilemma is how alert to life are we? Are we savouring every moment as though it's our last or are we listlessly sleepwalking through our days, marking time?

Mindful breathing uses the breath as an object of focus and concentration. The simple practice of calm, deep, rhythmical breathing anchors us to the present moment. Becoming aware of our breath stops our mind from fluttering about and has a beneficial effect on our physical and mental state. It is an effective antidote to the emotional upheaval that torments us when somebody we love dies. Mindful breathing helps us to relax, and, once soothed, accept difficulties that confront us.

Awareness of breath reveals itself as a kiss of life. It gently stirs us back into full consciousness and opens our eyes to the wonders all around. Filling our lungs and being aware that we are breathing is fundamental to the essence of mindfulness.

DANCING WITH THE DEAD

◆

The dead never leave us. They remain in our consciousness, and our hearts, forever. When grieving, we should not endeavour to forget the people we love but rather, discover new ways of remembering and holding them close inside.

WHEN WE LOSE SOMEONE WE LOVE through death, we yearn for that person to come back. It's hard to take in the news. There is a feeling of absence and of wanting to find them again, even though we know the search is futile. We must learn how to turn towards such difficult thoughts, to manage and accept them – and in so doing, gradually progress psychologically towards the light at the end of our deeply shaded tunnel. Instead of being crippled and frozen by such thoughts and feelings, mindfulness brings insight into our emotional state, boosts our focus and ability to concentrate, and delivers tender, beneficial effects to our minds as we search for new meaning. By staying receptive to the realities of life – difficult as well as pleasurable – and allowing ourselves to embrace the here-and-now, we can learn to dance with the dead in a way that allows us to flourish.

There is a feeling of absence and of wanting to find them again.

Recovery is not about 'moving on', 'letting go', 'getting over it' or 'leaving it behind' – it is about accepting and

The Mindfulness Breakthrough

Mindfulness-Based Cognitive Therapy (MBCT) is a therapy designed to combat anxiety, depression and chronic unhappiness.[8] Once a misconceived New Age fad, mindfulness meditation has moved from the margins to the mainstream. MBCT combines the ideas of cognitive therapy with Eastern meditation techniques and attitudes. Participants develop the capacity to allow distressing moods, thoughts and sensations to come and go without fighting them. It enables us to stay in touch with the present moment and our current experience.

MBCT is neither psychobabble nor an alternative health therapy without substance. It is recommended in the UK by the National Institute for Health and Clinical Excellence (NICE) as the treatment of choice for preventing depressive relapse. It offers a positive alternative to antidepressant medication.[9]

Many systems of modern psychotherapy and counselling incorporate aspects of mindfulness into their practice, though often it is not labelled as such. The goal of MBCT is to perceive and pay attention, objectively, to the conditions of our mind and body that give rise to conflict – and then embrace whatever happens, as it occurs.

Mindfulness teaches us how to nurture and take care of ourselves and can be a transformative self-help tool when struggling with the trauma of bereavement.

adapting to a different reality and integrating the memory of the person who has died positively into our lives going forwards. Death is permanent and unchangeable but the processes of acclimatizing and constructing new connections with our departed one are gradual and ongoing. Remember, the spirits of the dead survive in the hearts of the living.

Coming to Terms with Death

I come to this book not as a Buddhist or therapist but as a trained Bereavement Volunteer working with a UK bereavement charity. I talk to and support grief-stricken clients face to face in their homes and I facilitate bereavement groups – something I've done for many years. Their loss might be recent, or have occurred thirty years ago, but the common thread is adjusting and coming to terms with death. I bear witness to their moving testimonies and allow my clients time to share their innermost feelings of loss and despair. Together, we examine strategies for surviving the turbulent waves of distress, without drowning.

All of us experience grief at some time or other but nothing can quite prepare us for how it feels. Grief is our fear of loss, our fear of the unknown, our fear of our own mortality. The excruciating pain of grief feels like rope burns left behind after somebody we love is pulled out from our grasp, but even the deepest and most agonizing wounds mend given time. The remarkable way in which my clients have faced bereavement

is a testament to their courage, the strength of the human spirit and our phenomenal capacity for healing. Their courageous journeys are those of inspiration and hope.

Recovery occurs slowly and on many levels: physical, psychological and spiritual. If we are to be wholly restored after a death we must learn to let go and greet the present fully, moment by moment. Everybody can discover this source of healing because, potentially, it lies within us all.

I Am Not There

Do not stand at my grave and weep,

I am not there, I do not sleep.

I am a thousand winds that blow.

I am the diamond glints on snow.

I am the sunlight on ripened grain.

I am the gentle autumn rain.

When you awaken in the morning's hush

I am the swift uplifting rush

Of quiet birds in circled flight.

I am the soft stars that shine at night.

Do not stand at my grave and cry;

I am not there, I did not die.

OLD INDIAN BURIAL PRAYER
ANON

Journey's End

Each individual's expedition of bereavement is unique: some are becalmed; some frightened; others full of anger, guilt and remorse. There is no general template of grief to offer up and no universal remedy. There is simply an unknown voyage on which each of us is compelled to travel. There is no schedule or shared itinerary. What is unquestionable is that recognizing and accepting our true feelings – the practice of mindfulness – will make our journey more bearable and restorative.

A journey of a thousand miles begins with a single step. Following a death, we must brace ourselves, breathe in deeply and gently take one step forwards if we are to mend ourselves. Grief is not an illness to overcome but a process of steadily reconstructing meaning. Bereavement is a challenging but natural human experience from which it is possible to emerge, recover and stand upright again to face the future and our new realities.[10]

The sun rises in spite of everything

and the far cities are beautiful and bright.

I lie here in a riot of sunlight

watching the day break and the clouds flying.

Everything is going to be all right.

FROM 'EVERYTHING IS GOING TO BE ALL RIGHT'
DEREK MAHON, *NEW COLLECTED POEMS* (THE GALLERY PRESS, 2011)[11]

THE MERCY OF MINDFULNESS

◆

Bereavement can feel like a dead weight — solid, a heaviness that threatens to eclipse our lives; yet grief is also a common thread that binds humanity. Losing a loved one feels unbearable and yet, mostly, we bear our sorrow and face the day. Willingness to accept the pain of loss eventually melts into mercy and relief.

I HAVE MY OWN HARROWING STORIES of bereavement to share. Both my parents died through suicide: my father when I was twenty-one and my mother twelve years later. For many years I refused to understand or forgive them and buried myself in work and anger. I didn't allow myself to grieve because I could feel their deaths only through my own wounds. I felt angry towards them for what they had done to me — for the deep traumatic scars with which they had burdened their family, and for abandoning me. I didn't understand their pain or the destructive nature of their relationship and I was too absorbed in my own situation to understand or be able to forgive theirs.

After my father's suicide I was so blinded by rage that I couldn't grieve. I cried once and then covered my emotions with a sticking plaster of frenetic activity. It held my wounds together but they didn't heal. By contrast, the suicide of my mother was so overwhelming that it was impossible to hide from or suppress my emotions any longer. Her death was my

catalyst for change. I surrendered. I finally allowed myself to grieve for them both in such a way that eased, and then gradually, resolved my torment.

Learning to Let Go

Over time I learned to let go of anger and accept my relationship with my parents for what it was. Once I embraced the realities, let go of my struggle and allowed things to be just as they were, my feelings changed and I was able to bring them back into my life more positively. The gap between how we would like things to be and the way things are is one of life's conundrums. Focusing on the differences and wishing it were otherwise leads to anxiety and undermines our joy in life.

My cure was to become aware of the contrasts and to accept them. In seeing this gap through new eyes, I was able to bridge it. Things were as they were. Instead of focusing on what my parents took away, I focused on what they gave me. Instead of feeling angry and aggressive, I took them back into my heart with love and understanding. Mindfulness invites us to challenge painful feelings in a generous and open-hearted way and, by so doing, something merciful will happen.

Awareness & Transformation

Through awareness, transformation becomes possible. Buddhism teaches that suffering is a natural part of life and that

our path to happiness begins with an understanding and acceptance of this universal truth. There should be no denying or hiding away from suffering or the daily tragedies of life but at the same time it is possible to accept these formidable certainties and still enjoy peace and contentment.

Mindfulness is the tool that helps train our minds not to live in the past or future but to live fully in the here-and-now. When we are bereaved, we need to allow ourselves time for grief to run its natural course. We then need to let go of the sadness and face our future again

Hope is our fountain-head.

positively. As long as there is life, there is hope. As long as there is hope, there is life. Hope is our fountain-head.

The Grief Cycle

When considering how best to explore the benefits of mindfulness during our struggle with bereavement, I decided to adopt the model of 'normal grief' first proposed by Elisabeth Kübler-Ross (1926–2004) as my skeleton. In her 1969 book *On Death and Dying*, inspired by working with the terminally ill, Kübler-Ross writes about the emotional stages that we experience when faced with life-altering events such as the death of somebody close. While her theories are not universally embraced, she arguably defined the clinical field of care for those suffering loss and bereavement and, in effect, pioneered the modern hospice movement.[12]

Dying is something we human beings do continuously,
not just at the end of our physical lives on earth.

FROM 'DEATH: THE FINAL STAGE OF GROWTH'
ELISABETH KÜBLER-ROSS, 1975 [13]

Kübler-Ross understood that when talking to the bereaved or those facing death, it was important to walk sensitively alongside them in their struggle without appearing superficial and patronizing, or offering unsolicited advice. It was important to listen and empathize fully with their needs.

Her hypothesis argues that bereavement, loss and grief are natural and universal, and that there are five emotional stages that we have to work through in order to achieve a more peaceful acceptance of death. These are: *Denial*; *Anger*; *Bargaining*; *Depression*; *Acceptance*.

Also known as 'The Grief Cycle', these five stages are not linear, nor are they equal in their intensity. They ebb and flow like the tide rather than sweeping in sequentially; they get revisited; they occur in different orders and time frames; they vary from person to person and, indeed, we may not even experience them at all. These individual phases of grief can last for hours, weeks or years as we flow in and out of one and back into another. There is no set pattern or formula for charting progress: our grief and our reactions to death are as individual to us as a fingerprint.

Understanding our Sorrow

Kübler-Ross never intended her model to be a prescriptive template – rather a way of humanizing the process of death and creating a concept that reveals what is happening to us during bereavement.[14] Her proposition explains the pattern of emotional adjustment we need to make in order to recover ourselves after a death. We are not going insane, nor are we sick – we've lost somebody central to our life, suffered a trauma and are grief-stricken. It is a natural human process that we all experience at some point in our lives, which takes time to work through and resolve.

Grief is only part of the emotional response to our journey through loss. It is not the totality. Many of us are robust enough to be able to work our way through bereavement alone. Others need to explore and talk through unresolved issues in the relationship to find tranquillity. Grief often manifests itself through negative feelings such as self-judgement, fear, anger, guilt and blame. It brings with it a tendency to cling and condemn and is often accompanied by a deep sense of isolation and separation.

The gradual acceptance of where we find ourselves allows us to feel what we feel. Some deaths are violent, others more peaceful; but when confronted with loss, we each have to understand our needs, focus our full attention on our reactions, and be ready to embrace the new realities that present themselves in our lives.

The Grief Cycle model brings helpful insights to reading and interpreting our emotional states. The key to understanding the different stages of grief is recognizing there is no norm: we may experience some or all of them and they strike randomly, in no precise order. Kübler-Ross's hypothesis was a simple way of translating the complexities of what might be occurring emotionally. When we understand what is happening to us, dealing with it becomes much easier.

During mourning we feel lost and detached. Our faith in life disappears into a pit of gloom, nothingness. Despite this, we should allow ourselves to react naturally to our loss, not close down or try to turn away from difficult emotions. This will help to normalize our feelings, however volatile. Mindfulness invites us to turn towards and face what we are experiencing, however hard, and to accept our suffering – because to do otherwise is pointless.

If we develop open-mindedness towards the problems we encounter and become receptive to our senses moment by moment, we will better survive our bereavement. Every second we participate fully in life, step by step, breath by breath, will deepen our understanding and potential for rebuilding ourselves.

The key to understanding the different stages of grief is recognizing there is no norm.

Active Listening

Sometimes, the most valuable gift in the world is a listening ear. To feel the love and concern of somebody who allows us to say anything, without judgement or wanting us to be different — who really hears what we say — can be a life-saver. Mindfulness teaches us to listen to our own voice as well as others'.

Mindfulness and the Journey of Bereavement explores beneficial ways of coming to terms with loss. Each of the five chapters that follow takes one of the emotional stages of grief that Kübler-Ross described and shows how mindfulness can bring fresh perspectives to our suffering. We will discover new things about ourselves and, through our enriched self-knowledge, find helpful techniques to alter the way we experience death and suffering. Mindful exercise will help us recover — regenerating and restoring hope.

My work as a bereavement counsellor exposes me to countless stories of death and the earth-shattering aftermath that follows in its wake. Not all the bereaved need counselling or support, by any means; but for those who do, I listen sensitively and without judgement to their touching stories. For a short time I enter their world and, together, we explore ways in which they might reconcile their feelings. I walk alongside them for part of their solitary journey, offering a safe, empathetic and neutral space in which to reflect,

investigate and hopefully make peace with their sources of torment. This approach is called 'active listening'.[15]

An Unparalleled Experience

To illustrate the diverse range of emotions any of us may encounter during grief, I recount some of those moving testaments here. I bring them to life in a way that respects my clients' confidentiality and privacy, while acknowledging the privilege I was granted in bearing witness to their misery in our weekly sessions.

These 'client vignettes' are used to explore particular responses to death. Each describes the death endured and the suffering experienced as a consequence. Remember, each story is one person's unique reaction to the loss of a special relationship with another human being. No two pictures are identical. The colour of my life is exclusive to me. The colour of yours is without equal. Faced with similar circumstances to those described, our reactions would each be different.

How we respond to death varies a great deal. Some of us are naturally more resilient than others but every experience of grief is unmatched. Like much of life, grieving is a process with no predictable trajectory or outcome. We mourn and cherish our loved ones; we miss them continually – but usually our wounds mend well enough for us to forge new relationships, make peace with our pain, discover new meaning and continue on our life's journey.

Emerging From Grief, Reborn

Strong social networks and family and friends undoubtedly assist us on our journey through bereavement but they don't lessen the pain of loss. The suffering is just as intense – despite help being on hand to support a fall. Following a death, the world around us carries on as normal but we feel separated from it – encased in a bubble of pain and isolation, a world apart. Unfortunately, we are on our own with grief. Physical or mental illness, especially depression, may delay our recovery but the remedy is down to us. Be mindful, breathe slowly, fill your lungs and move forwards; it is possible to emerge from grief reborn.

Remember, emotions are not separate – they dance together side by side. One day we perhaps feel consumed by guilt and remorse; the next, sad but optimistic. Our feelings fluctuate in a melody of continual movement, twisting and turning, never constant, always changing. Be patient; don't expect a bump-free journey. Allow yourself to experience the emotional turbulence of grief fully, without self-judgement.

◆

'People are like stained-glass windows.
They sparkle and shine when the sun is out, but
when the darkness sets in, their true beauty is revealed
only if there is a light from within.'

ELISABETH KÜBLER-ROSS

◆

33

Being mindful of the moment is to experience whatever we are feeling completely; to embrace and savour the taste of every second as though it might be our last. It's naïve to believe we can always participate fully with the present, without dredging up the past or ruminating about the future – especially when the present is frightening and traumatic. Accepting suffering is hard. Allowing ourselves to look those emotions squarely in the eye, without blinking, feels impossible – but there is no healthier, realistic alternative.

Mindfulness can help each of us restore hope in ourselves and in life following a death. It will gently open our eyes to new possibilities for the future and shine a soothing light on to our battle with bereavement. We will discover that it is possible to dig deep within ourselves, into our hearts and minds, and draw on hidden reserves. Once revealed, this inner strength may well become the fertile seeds of a new beginning.

The first step is to absorb the basic message of mindfulness so that we are better equipped to face death and adjust to life without our loved one. The roots of counteracting stress using mindfulness-based techniques were planted by Jon Kabat-Zinn in the 1970s and laid bare in his groundbreaking work 'Full Catastrophe Living', published in 1990, in which he describes our ability to get to grips with what is most difficult in life, in ourselves, and to grow in strength. He distilled Seven Foundations of Mindfulness (abbreviated opposite) as an effective antidote for calming fear, anxiety and panic.[16]

1. Non-judging: we cultivate mindfulness by assuming the stance of an impartial witness to our own experience and by just observing it.

2. Patience: a form of wisdom; it demonstrates that we understand and accept the fact that things must unfold in their own time.

3. Beginner's mind: cultivating a mind that is willing to see everything as if for the first time. No moment is the same as any other.

4. Trust: developing a basic trust in ourselves. Learning to live our own lives, taking responsibility for being ourselves, listening to and trusting in our own feelings.

5. Non-striving: almost everything we do, we do for a purpose – to get something or to get somewhere. In meditation this can be an obstacle because meditation is non-doing. It has no goal other than to be ourselves.

6. Acceptance: a willingness to see things as they actually are at the present moment, allowing them to be so.

7. Letting go: cultivating the attitude of letting things go; non-attachment is fundamental to the practice of mindfulness.

'We can't stop the waves but we can learn how to surf.'

FROM 'MINDFULNESS MEDITATION FOR EVERYDAY LIFE'
JON KABAT-ZINN

1. MINDFULNESS FOR MAINSTREAM MEDICINE

Two heroic healers loom large in our story of grief, hope and restoration – both responsible, in their different ways, for bringing mindfulness into the mainstream, transforming lives.

• **Thich Nhat Hanh** – an exiled Vietnamese Zen spiritual leader, teacher, inspirational peace and human rights activist, brought the practice of Mindfulness to the wider attention of a western audience in the late 1960s. Affectionately known to his followers as 'Thay' (Vietnamese for master or teacher), his lifelong mission of advocating Buddhist principles of non-violence and compassionate action around the world is profound.[17]

• **Jon Kabat-Zinn** – an American molecular biologist with an interest in Buddhism, developed Mindfulness-Based Stress Reduction (MBSR), a fusion of Western medicine and Eastern meditation, during the 1970s. He demonstrated radical methods for counteracting stress, achieving much greater body/mind balance, harmony and healing. His enduring, medically proven programme planted deep roots in a whole new field of medicine and psychology. It offers us the harvest of living nourishing, more authentic lives if we respond to life's challenges with a greater sense of understanding and compassion for ourselves and others.

2. **BEING PRESENT**

When we are fully in the present, it is easier to see how we are living, to be more aware of the choices we make and thus develop a contented, better quality of life. If we can achieve this we will gain more satisfaction from many of the things to which we might otherwise never have given a second thought.[18]

In order to become mindful, we need to *practise* being mindful. We are not trying to stop ourselves thinking; we are simply learning how to engage with our senses, without the distractions of the past or future. Our first step is learning how to breathe and relax. This is best done, initially, on our own, quietly, for periods of four or five minutes.

1. Sit comfortably in a chair and gently close your eyes. Sit upright, back straight, unsupported, your legs hip-width apart and your feet placed squarely and evenly on the floor, directly below your knees.

2. Rest your forearms on your thighs, with your hands open or clasped together in front – whatever feels most comfortable. Relax.

3. Allow yourself to experience whatever it is you are feeling. Notice your breath, your feelings and physical sensations; mentally scan and explore how your mind and body feels – without analysis or guilt – gaining a true sense of what's going on within yourself right now.

4. Breathe normally but bring your attention to your breath, focusing on one single aspect – perhaps the sensation of air passing through a nostril or the rising and falling movements in your chest.

5. Concentrating on a single element of the breath allows us to be present with our feelings. Breathing in; breathing out. Allow your awareness to expand, following your breath, slightly softer, allowing your whole body to open up and breathe.

6. When you are ready, gently open your eyes.

CHAPTER ONE

DENIAL

*My second bereavement, the suicide
of my mother, knocked me to the floor.
Her death was crushing, life-changing. I was
thirty-three, enjoying a happy relationship and a
successful career in publishing. I denied my distress as
best I could but inside I was tormented by grief and
emotionally unsteady. It took ten years to calm the
storm and see the other side of the coin — restoration.
On New Year's Day 1994, I walked into my local
Samaritans branch and volunteered. I felt ready to
accept myself, warts and all; to embrace my
parents and use all that suffering in
a more rewarding way.*

DECEIVING OURSELVES

◆

Denial is the rejection of truth: a resistance to reason. It is a false belief held in the face of evidence to the contrary. It is a delusion, a fallacy, a deception. Denial is often our first response to being told that somebody we love has died.

IMMERSED IN OUR CULTURAL AVERSION TO DEATH, many of us choose to turn away from life's impermanence, ignoring reality. Death is easily denied. Even if, at the moment of death, we're with our loved one, holding their hand because we're frightened of letting them go, our overriding sense is still one of disbelief. Our mind recoils at losing what it loves – but if death is faced with honesty, it can greatly increase our insight and ultimately, our recovery.

Physical and emotional attachment to another person is a natural human instinct we all share, and grief the natural response to being parted from those we love. When somebody dear to us dies, we relive the circumstances of their death – rerunning events, over and over.

This psychological replaying is linked to the trauma of loss and is one of the many mind/body reactions we might encounter. Sorrow manifests itself in numerous ways – physically, emotionally, mentally and behaviourally; thus we must stay alert to our condition, moment by moment, because the effects of bereavement can be bewildering and disorientating.

We tend to think of grief in terms of sadness and tears, so it may surprise us just how physical the pain of bereavement can be; how drained and exhausted it can make us feel.

Why Deny Death?

The denial of death is an elaborate psychological defence mechanism – self-protection, if you like – against the pain and knowledge of our own fragile mortality. Death is a sad, painful, often bloody business – so yes, of course we prefer to deny it. Vigour and Youth persuade us to feel invincible, immortal. We imagine life going on forever, believing we will never be separated from those we love. We feel in control of life – but we're not. All of us come from the same source and will eventually return to it. The death of somebody close undermines the certainty of our supremacy and shakes the very foundations of our existence.

We feel in control of life – but we're not.

We want to hold on to our life and to all those we love. Death, when it occurs, feels cruel and unfair, inhumane and wasteful. Why did this have to happen to me? It seems inconceivable. Death no longer feels abstract but deeply personal; it makes us think about life and interrogates our beliefs. Some of us may draw comfort and strength from faith; others go through a period of searching and questioning. One of the deepest expressions of loss lies in our struggle to find an answer or explanation that makes any sense.

The Remedy

The antidote to denial is learning to experience reality as it truly is. We must turn and face reality; we must look reality directly in the eyes, unblinkingly. Life is a fluctuation of joy and sadness. They are both natural and inseparable. Like birth, illness or old age, death is yet another event along the way. It is nothing unusual. Death is ordinary and democratic; it comes to us all. Each phase of life is born and then dies. Without our preconditioned anxieties of desire, fear and expectation, we can free ourselves from denial. But we must look to ourselves for such healing and reflect on what we, as individuals, need in order to restore hope.

We are never prepared for what grief feels like: the fear; the emptiness and dread; the agony; the rivers of unending tears; the silence; the isolation and the dreadful sense of separation. In the first days after the death of someone close, most of us feel stunned, numb, almost concussed. We cannot believe they have gone and we are lost in a fog of confusion. 'This was the one person I never imagined not being in my

---

'Your vision will become clear only when you
look into your own heart. Who looks outside,
dreams; who looks inside, awakens.'

CARL JUNG (1875–1961)
PSYCHIATRIST & PSYCHOTHERAPIST

---

life any more.' Denial of death is our refusal, our inability, to take in and accept the fact. Life without our loved one there beside us feels unbearable and makes no sense; our minds are bursting with dread and turmoil and we are thrown into a traumatized state of shock and disbelief.

We think about the person who has died all the time and wonder how we can possibly survive or go on without them. Emotionally, we block out the words of death; we don't want to hear their bleak finality; we cover our ears; we cry out; we hide from the truth. Denial accompanies us through the first terrible waves of bereavement and perhaps is nature's way of rationing out the shock so we're not completely crushed.

Facing Up to Death

The reality of a loved one dying is so catastrophic that our mind disowns the event. We want to sweep it away and pretend it hasn't happened. We refuse to absorb it. We reject the truth of death in favour of something kinder – and who can blame us? Death feels cruel, icy and final. When a loved one is lost, we lose a connection with ourselves.

Sometimes we delude ourselves into believing the person is still alive, that they're coming back, they're in the room next door. We think we've seen and smelled them – and we may be convinced we have: we talk to the dead long after they've departed. For us they are not dead at all but vividly alive in our heads and hearts. They were here only a short time ago; how can they possibly be gone forever? The loss is so unacceptable that we deny the facts. But if we delude ourselves then we are hiding away from the truth. Mindfulness shows us how to manage difficult emotions and face reality.

Understanding our Grief

Death is shockingly final and facing loss is one of our deepest human challenges. We shake our heads, renounce the facts, and reject the truth. We know our loved one is dead, absent, and yet nothing will persuade us that they have simply vanished. How do we accept that the person we want most, we can no longer have? The pain of loss feels intolerable, as though part of us is missing. There are no shortcuts around death or grief. The only way forwards is through the middle.

As discussed, Elisabeth Kübler-Ross developed her theory that, after bereavement, we move backwards and forwards through five stages of grief towards acceptance. In 1982, American psychologist J. William Worden encouraged a more active approach to recovery. He specified *four specific tasks* of mourning that we must accomplish before we can adjust to a changed world, assimilate new realities and move forwards with our lives. *Task 1* was to accept the reality of loss; *task 2* was to experience the pain of grief; *task 3* was to adjust to an environment in which the deceased is absent; and *task 4* was to withdraw emotional energy from the deceased and reinvest it in other social activity, without uncertainty or guilt.

Neither Kübler-Ross's five-stage nor Worden's four-task models were ever intended to be seen as rigid or invariable blueprints. Rather, they were insights into the physical sensations and mental processes that might be happening within. In a similar way, mindfulness invites us to turn and face the truth and look inside ourselves, awake, with eyes wide open. It helps us interrogate our emotions with clarity and truth. We may detest our insights but at least, in seeing, we can no longer deny the fact that our loved one has gone.

TERMINAL ILLNESS & PRE-BEREAVEMENT

The knowledge that somebody we hold dear is suffering from a terminal illness can leave us feeling devastated, angry and powerless. When the end finally arrives, hopefully, it will be peaceful and dignified. Unfortunately, death is not always calm and controlled.

SOMETIMES DEATH CAN BE SLOW, TORTUROUS, brutal and undignified, full of fear and denial. Everyday life comes to a standstill while nursing a loved one, and afterwards it can be difficult picking up the threads of normal life again. Indeed, the terrible experience of watching a loved one die can be so gruelling that, for a long time, it might be hard to shake free of the memory. We may feel haunted by their slow decline or upset at changes in the relationship brought about by their illness. And when death finally comes, though perhaps relieved that the suffering is over (theirs and ours), we will be left feeling grief-stricken, exhausted and alone – perhaps wishing we could have done more. Old landmarks will have vanished and our personal landscape changed forever.

Saying Goodbye

Despite being profoundly testing, incurable disease at least provides opportunities for saying goodbye and preparing for death. We can make ready for the impending loss and, as each change happens, grieve little by little for what's slipping away. Some of us are able to talk about dying, and this will be made easier if we accept the end is approaching. Others will find conversations like this impossible, so it's unrealistic trying to change the habits of a lifetime and talk to those we love as never before. But whatever is said or left unsaid between loved ones, much is understood without the need for words.

For the patient, it is their unique chance to have their dying wishes met, and for the caregiver, a valuable time to discover what really matters at the end of life. We only live once; we only die once. Dying is important – after all, it is our final act of living. But how do we prepare ourselves for this last act? How do we accept our condition? How do we examine death without becoming paralysed by fear, without denial, paying full attention to the passing from life to death?

With incurable diagnosis comes the crushing realization that time is running out. Everything changes. Our own mortality feels closer. The balance of generations shifts around and we perhaps question where we are in our own life. With our physical bonds on the verge of breaking, mutual mourning kicks in hard as we make ready for separation and loss.

Unfinished Business

Grieving begins even while our loved one is still alive, and will continue long after they've gone. Waves of sorrow wash over us and yet we may also feel frustrated by unfinished business in the relationship. It's a significant and desperate time. Caregivers grieve for the loss of the person they were before they became guardians; patients grieve for wasted time and lost opportunities. Both grieve for what is slipping away and all the things that could have been said or done differently.

One of the greatest sorrows of death is realizing that it is too late to say 'sorry' or to change things. We may experience intense feelings of regret, bitterness or anger over unresolved issues, but whatever has happened in the past is done with and can now never be altered or put right. We must learn to forgive ourselves and our loved ones and let go. The English poet-artist William Blake's ecstatic vision of the universe is one in which 'every particle of dust breathes forth its joy.' In death we must treasure joys, accept what is lost and gain strength from the full experience of life and death. The joy of loving another human being, and the knowledge of what they mean to us, remains part of us for the rest of our lives.

DEATH CAFES & DOULAS

◆

The first, most important event in all our lives is our birth; the second, our death. But how many of us are ready to die when death approaches? What about the loose ends and all our unlived life? Still so much to do…

MINDFULNESS TEACHES us that life becomes a more authentic and satisfying experience by concentrating on the here-and-now, rather than being sidetracked by the past or future. It helps us see the futility of allowing our minds to wander and be anywhere other than where we are. Relishing the present moment, without distraction, helps us to be fully awake to every encounter with life, rather than absent.

Dying is the inescapable and universal end to the adventure of living. It is our last activity in life and a momentous one – an event that many have difficulty talking about let alone acknowledging. In the West, death has become a clinical matter, a medical failure to be angry about, rather than a natural conclusion to a life well lived and a final act of existence.

Approaching Death

None of us knows the nature of death or what it feels like until we experience it for ourselves. We may have encountered death, vicariously, through others but we haven't tasted it firsthand. The idea that someday we will not be here

DENIAL

anymore is difficult to imagine. Mindfulness may teach us to focus on the present but, even so, it's still hard not to think about death and dying. When our time comes, will we be frightened, feel pain or be calm and accepting? We don't know; all we can do is stay aware of life as we live it and surrender to whatever unfolds. At the end, some of us will want to be comforted and stroked as we pass away, others, to walk towards death with eyes wide open – to die fully alive.

We each have finite time to make the most of all of our living moments right up until we draw our very last breath. My Buddhist friend Ngak'chang Rinpoche observes, 'We eventually discover that joy and sorrow have one taste.' Being human is a fluctuation of both emotions. When considering mortality, our own or that of those we love, we must accept death as a natural process from which there is no hiding place. Dying is as much a part of life as living.

Helping Hands

There are many ways of making ourselves more comfortable with the notion of dying: Cruse Bereavement Care[19] and similar organizations around the world offer support to the bereaved or those about to be, while global movements such as Death Cafe[20] increase awareness of death – helping us to make the most of life. Death Cafe creates welcoming, open spaces for people with a curiosity or wish to explore the universal experience of death and dying. Strangers meet together, eat cake, drink tea and discuss mortality without agenda, objectives or themes, casting light into the dark and reminding us of the importance of living our lives to the full.

Belief in another life after death can be a comforting prospect for some but my focus is this life – here and now. The charity 'Living Well Dying Well'[21] is pioneering the use of Death Doulas. These are people who support individuals and families through the process of dying, offering end-of-life mentoring and companionship. Hardly a new idea but perhaps a kinder and more holistic approach to death than our twenty-first-century sterilized alternative. It encourages an approach to dying that is humane and respectful – one that honours a person's identity and sense of self. Mostly, we prefer to die at home, in familiar surroundings, cared for lovingly by friends and family – rather than slipping from life in a hospital ward full of stress and strangers. Doulas assist in this journey. But as none of us know what death is, or the nature of its coming, perhaps dying is nothing to fear after all?

'Those who have the strength and the love to sit with a
dying patient in the silence that goes beyond words will know that
this moment is neither frightening nor painful, but a peaceful
cessation of the functioning of the body.'

FROM 'ON DEATH AND DYING'
ELISABETH KÜBLER-ROSS, 1969

Letters to a Loved One

Saying things in death that we wanted to say in life, but never did, can bring closure to unresolved difficulties in the relationship. Seeing the words in black and white; writing them down; speaking them aloud and posting them to the wind may help our grieving. Mindfulness allows us to acknowledge feelings of bitterness and resentment then lay them aside.

Speaking with the dead is a therapeutic way of communing with our loved ones. It preserves them emotionally in our hearts and minds. It's neither morbid nor unusual to want to maintain a link with somebody we love, one who has been woven deeply into the fabric of our everyday life. There will be no replies, no answers – only those of our imagination – but the process of unburdening and confronting this outpouring will free us of the emotional baggage that weighs us down and pulls us back from recovery.

Rather than locking grief away in a drawer full of denial and despair, we should learn to experience it fully. The first step on our journey of healing is acceptance. We must receive the truth, not reject it. We must accept our emotions, face on, however hard. We cannot go backwards in life, only forwards. The act of writing a letter, expressing our true feelings, liberates our thoughts, transforming our words into those of regeneration, acceptance and reconciliation.

ANNE'S STORY

ANNE was fixed solidly in denial. She was unable to accept the reality of her parents' death, especially her mother's, and, set solid like cement, she could move neither backwards nor forwards with her life.

Anne was in her fifties, single, and had always lived contentedly at home. Her father had died decades earlier and her mother, four years before she started coming to the bereavement group. When Anne first attended she was suffering a panic attack. She had difficulty in breathing; she looked petrified, was sweating and could hardly speak. She cried inconsolably and said she had nothing to live for.

Anne and her mother had been best friends and companions throughout her entire life and they did everything together. Her mother was the dominant driving force and made all the decisions – which suited them both. When Anne was made redundant, they settled into closed, mutually beneficial patterns of shopping, drives into the country, time at home, trips to the theatre, meals out together, time spent with a handful of old friends.

Everything ended abruptly when her mother died in hospital of a seizure, at the age of ninety. She had lived a long life. Anne was furious with the hospital for allowing her mother to die. She was inconsolable. She felt she had lost everything of meaning and significance.

Anne was marooned alone in the large family house. She had a younger married sister whom she saw on occasions but they weren't particularly close. When their mother died, her sister wanted her half of the inheritance and so the house was put up for sale. Anne didn't want to leave. Why would she, it was her home – she had always lived there, where would she go? She was too disturbed and distraught to express any resistance so instead, conceded.

Traumatized, depressed and frozen in denial, Anne packed her entire home into boxes ready for the move. This, however, was as far as she got. She refused to look at other houses or allow anyone to view hers. She was stuck where she wanted to stay. Her relationship with her sister deteriorated as her sibling grew increasingly angry at what she saw as bloody-minded obstinacy, and Anne became intransigent and isolated.

Anne's main trip out was a weekly visit to the churchyard every Sunday, where she went to tend her parents' grave. She spent time there planting flowers, tidying up the plot, talking to her mother, asking for advice and berating her for leaving. Apart from that, Anne's life consisted of local food shopping, appointments with her doctor (who was genuinely caring) and attending my bereavement group. She refused to see a psychiatrist and only told her doctor what she thought he wanted to hear. At the group she spoke of only ever leaving the house in a box and of longing to join her parents. Anne denied the new realities of her situation completely and refused to consider change. She felt she had absolutely nothing left to live for because every day without her mother was another full of isolation, despair and terror.

Summary

Anne came to the group every week for two years but struggled to find purpose. I have no way of knowing what became of her but I like to believe that her absence is a good sign, not a bad one.

CAROL'S STORY

CAROL looked bewildered – almost drunk. She kept drifting away, preoccupied. She was. She was listening out for Alan, her dead husband. Alan was seventy-eight when he slammed to the floor two months earlier with a massive heart attack. He was a big man and had probably gone before he hit the ground.

Carol stayed with him, holding his hand, talking to him, soothing him. She lay down next to Alan, hugging him, until the paramedics arrived. They did their best but he was pronounced dead. She travelled with Alan in the ambulance to the hospital and then waited with him until their daughter arrived three hours later. What were three hours after their fifty-seven years of marriage?

They met as teenagers when Alan stopped to help her up after a fall from her bicycle. Thereafter, he was life's stabilizer. He kept Carol balanced and she felt safe and secure, upright and steady with him.

They raised two children together and, for the last twenty years, worked together managing a holiday park. Alan was the practical 'fixer' – dashing here and there on his quad bike. Carol was the park organizer and responsible for taking the bookings. Together they made a wonderful team. They didn't smother in each other's pockets but overlapped like two comfortable blankets, wrapped warm and secure in the knowledge that they had each other.

When Alan died, Carol spent every morning at the undertakers, talking to him, making funeral arrangements, being with him, laying with him. She could see he was dead but somehow, she kept expecting him to be there when she got home. Bereavement isn't a rational companion. Alan might be alive; he could be out there somewhere fixing a fence? These thoughts of denial gave her comfort and helped her survive each day.

She carried on working during the early stages of grief but, without Alan, everything felt meaningless. Her emotional stabilizers were crushed and she toppled, just as she had done all those years earlier when Alan first came to the rescue. Carol felt broken and beaten. The reality of the funeral and the presence of her family and friends didn't stop her from expecting Alan to walk through the door at any moment. Locked firmly into her denial, Carol shrank back from the reality of impermanence. Denial was more tolerable.

These thoughts of denial gave her comfort and helped her survive each day.

Summary

Carol decided to stop our sessions. She acknowledged they were helpful but what she most wanted was to meet other widows in similar circumstances. To this end, she formed a local friendship group to meet for walks and social outings. Carol was beginning to build her new future.

3. A GOOD NIGHT'S SLEEP

Sleep is as essential to our health and well-being as food, air and water. Sleep is restorative, calming, and yet, when we're bereaved (already dog-tired and desperately exhausted), the harder we try to sleep, the more elusive sleep seems to become.

In the wake of a death, all too often our regular bedfellows are insomnia, fatigue, nightmares, sleep deprivation and chronic sleep disturbance. Sleep Hygiene means ensuring that even during the despair of loss, we do everything possible to gift ourselves the healing grace of a good night's sleep. This exercise focuses on creating a comforting, ambient, sleeping space.

1. Ensure your bed is comfortable, in a quiet room that is dark and warm enough to encourage sleep. A welcoming space.

2. Reinforce the connection between bed and sleep. Don't use the bedroom for waking activities such as work, watching television, surfing the net, texting or phone calls.

3. Clear the bedroom of all electronic gadgets. The light these devices emit, although subtle, makes it especially difficult to nod off.

4. Establish a bedtime routine/ritual to invite sleep: relax mentally and physically for an hour before turning in; reduce your intake of stimulants such as alcohol and caffeine; relax in a hot bath; make yourself a warm drink (milky, herbal tea, hot water, honey and lemon); go to bed when you feel tired, not before, and if you can't sleep, get up for a while. Rise at the same time each morning.

5. Allow yourself to settle; observe your breath; breathe deeply; notice it going in and out of your body; see what happens when you practise letting go of your desire to clear away your thoughts.

Mindfulness emphasizes that life is to be found in the present moment; try not to think about the past or future.

4. **FOOD FOR THOUGHT**

When somebody we love dies, it can be hard finding the will to eat but staying healthy speeds our recovery. Despite lack of motivation and the temptation to eat nothing or gulp down ready-made meals, we should eat nourishing food on a daily basis.

Over time, our appetite for life will return but in the meantime, cooking can be restorative, helpful in reconnecting us to our loved one – relishing good memories of life, once tasted together.

This practice will feed your mind and body, creating a daily ritual of celebration for the experience of living – nourishing fresh taste buds for new realities.

1. Decide what to eat; choose your raw ingredients carefully; pay attention and notice what you are selecting and buying; think about their long journey from the earth to the shop, to your plate.

2. Slow down as you prepare your meal; look at the food's colour and texture, how it feels to handle; be aware and conscious of all the careful work invested in its preparation. If you are still cooking food enough for two, that's okay, just put half aside to freeze later.

3. Lay the table; sit down quietly and eat your meal properly; enjoy the smell, taste and texture of the food; chew slowly and mindfully, without the distraction of television or a wandering mind. Be with your food, enjoy each mouthful, giving it the attention it deserves.

4. Preparing a meal for yourself may accentuate feelings of being alone. If you find yourself getting upset, looking at your loved one's empty chair, try sitting where they once sat. You might find it reassuring and it could alter your perspective.

Resist the self-flagellation of comfort eating, gorging on rubbish, craving too much salt, fat, sugar, or yearning hunger for your loved one. Feed yourself, not your pain.

CHAPTER TWO

ANGER

*During the fifteen years
I volunteered with Samaritans,
I observed struggle, despair, death and
rage in kaleidoscopic guises. Hearing callers,
listening empathetically and without judgement,
witnessing their emotional release, revealed the endless
promiscuity and turbulence of our human condition.
Supporting callers, many suicidal, lent deeper
insight into my own loss and illuminated the
perilous undercurrents that threaten everybody
swimming the river of life. Samaritan work taught
me that suffering is part of all our experience, and
while accepting this universal truth, it also
proclaimed the possibility of living a
happy, positive and hopeful life.*

WHAT IS ANGER?

Anger is the uncomfortable feeling of great annoyance, irritability, indignation or antagonism — usually as the result of some real or imagined grievance. Grief is a frightening, uncharted land and we want something to blame for the pain of our loss and separation.

ANGER IS AN INSTINCTIVE RESPONSE to the sense that somehow we have been offended, ill-treated or denied something we feel entitled to. When we experience rage, our natural response is to retaliate and strike out — either physically or verbally. Anger builds up inside us like a pressure cooker; either we try to suppress it or it explodes.

During times of mourning, anger can manifest itself in many ways. We want to attack; we want to blame — because we feel so terrible. 'Where is God in all this?' we rant. Sometimes we are angry with ourselves for not being able to prevent the death, or feel anger towards our loved one for dying and causing so much pain; we may be furious with the hospital or blame health professionals for not doing more, or we might simply *rage and fume* because we hurt so much ourselves; we may feel antagonistic towards neighbours for not expressing more sympathy or simply despise the world for turning normally while ours has been turned upside down.

It is completely natural to feel angry when somebody we love dies. Feeling hurt and alone makes us anxious and creates strong reactions that can spill over in outrage and acrimony towards everyone and everything. We need someone or something to blame for taking away and depriving us of the person we want most. At these times grief can feel like madness. The intense pain and raw emotion of loss can boil over in volcanic outbursts when we least expect it, shocking by their intensity. Choking back anguish, we know that our loved one didn't choose to leave us but that doesn't change how we feel.

A Slippery Foothold

By attributing blame, we direct our anger outwards towards others or we turn our anger inwards and blame ourselves. Sometimes we do both but neither is helpful. Anger constructs an imaginary bridge across the intensity of our sorrow but provides a perilously slippery foothold. Being angry feels tangible – something solid on which to harness our pain. Anger creates distraction, energy and focus and this can seem like a life-raft to cling on to while struggling to stay afloat in the sea of emptiness into which we're cast. But by centring on anger, we risk sinking.

◆

'Holding on to anger is like grasping a hot coal
with the intent of throwing it at someone else;
you are the one who gets burned.'

THE BUDDHA

◆

When we encounter explosive feelings, it is we who suffer most, tying ourselves up in knots of bitterness and resentment. Anger makes us feel frustrated, lowers self-esteem and then we spiral downwards. It is these responses that hold us hostage, making us prisoners of our own emotions, restricting our freedom to think clearly. Anger skews our reactions, blurs vision and dulls common sense, turning us into victims.

Working through toxic feelings is a part of the natural grieving process. Sometimes it is helpful to talk about how we feel with somebody neutral, who can listen and empathize. A sympathetic, honest ear and an outlet for expression is often all we need to help dissipate our anger and feel better.[22]

However, anger isn't always easy to recognize: sometimes it creeps up cleverly disguised as depression, fear or helplessness. But however anger and rage manifest themselves, beware! Whatever its guise, anger is poisonous and mostly counter-productive. It is far more cathartic to hold somebody with whom we're angry close to our hearts kindly and with compassion. This will liberate us from the prison of isolation and self-doubt that anger builds up around us.

The Remedy

The antidote to anger is loving-kindness and compassion – towards ourselves and to others. Remember, we shouldn't try to suppress or deny what we are experiencing; we should turn towards and acknowledge our feelings, accept them –

they are normal expressions of grief that need to be voiced and respected. Through employing mindfulness, of thought and feelings, we can learn to manage our mood better, clearing away the red mist of fury that often blinds us to reason.

Mindfulness is an invitation to see clearly and to use our anger constructively. We have a choice. If we do what we've always done, we get what we've always got. Our worst enemies do us less harm than our own self-destructive angry thoughts. We must resist being hijacked by knee-jerk reactions or lose sight of what we most want to achieve: to understand ourselves better; to make sense of how we feel and to find healthy solutions for improving our lives.

FAMILY SPLITS & RIFTS

A family is a complicated web of relationships in which, ideally, the strength of the group is greater than that of an individual member. Families are typically our main source of emotional and social support, albeit with intricate dynamics that either help or hinder our recovery following a death.

THE MAJORITY OF SIGNIFICANT BEREAVEMENTS that happen throughout our lives occur within the family. The day-to-day complexity of how each family member relates to another is delicate and elaborate – like a finely tuned instrument. When one member dies, it knocks the system off balance. The familiar, secure rhythms of the family unit are disrupted and members struggle to maintain their previous equilibrium.

In the wake of a family loss, roles get muddled up; responsibilities overlap and become blurred; established mechanisms grind to a halt. Although bereavement brings some families closer together, perversely, loss also magnifies underlying chasms and bitter conflict. Traumatic and irreversible change, such as death, can stir so much tension in the air that the reactions of the remaining family members, one to another, can become strained to breaking point.

Naïvely, we like to imagine family members all pulling together in a crisis, supportively, unified. But not all families are cohesive or caring and, sadly, not everybody has a happy childhood to look back on. There may have *Not all* been frequent rows, violence and neglect *families are* within the family, emotional coldness, death, *cohesive or* separation and divorce. There may be addiction issues, mental health problems or *caring.* unresolved family rifts. Parents may have parted, abandoned their children and established new lives with other families and different partners.

Some relationships are so damn complicated and dysfunctional that true forgiveness and healing are impossible while everyone is still alive. It might take the death of one or other of the participants to see the situation with clarity and wisdom.

Opening Up Old Wounds

Underlying feelings of anger towards parents, and jealousy and rivalry between siblings, can be the root of many long-standing resentments between family members. Death stirs up strong emotions, bringing powerful and suppressed feelings back to the surface – feelings of bitterness and acrimony that we believed were dead and buried or painful memories of separation and emotional turmoil that had been put to the back of our minds. When a death occurs, families can rupture, relationships snap, arguments and disagreements flare up and feelings smoulder. Rarely are family dynamics as strained and multi-layered as at the time of a death.

Parents are special. Mostly, they do their best by us but inevitably there are faults and failings on both sides which mindfulness can help acknowledge and accept. When a parent dies, we lose a link with our past that can never be regained. Sometimes though, if we are honest, the death of a parent may come as a relief. If the relationship has fractured, we may be at the end of our tether and just want to be free of the burden. Parents sometimes make unreasonable demands on their children, and vice versa, and yet, when one of them dies, old wounds reopen and we experience intense sorrow and regret that our relationship wasn't happier, more resolved.

Rarely are family dynamics as strained and multi-layered as at the time of a death.

In Their Shoes

Losing a much-loved member of a family can bring family chaos as well as grief. The feelings of surviving members are as different from each other as their fingerprints. Each member experiences the bereavement differently because every relationship to the deceased is distinct and unique. Remember, there are no blueprints to follow for how we should feel when somebody we love dies.

Try imagining how the death might be affecting other family members as well as yourself. Take ownership of your own pain and suffering but put yourself into other people's shoes as well as your own. See how they fit. Empathize with them. Imagine yourself over there with their feelings instead of being over here with yours. You might discover, surprisingly, that their emotions are totally at odds with your own – but don't judge them.

There are no blueprints to follow for how we should feel when somebody we love dies.

Such mindful practice helps us to handle the devastating challenges that loss brings to a family and to appreciate the diverse reactions experienced within the group. Mindfulness brings a non-judgemental acceptance to a situation, without attachment to any particular point of view, based on a solid foundation of peace, love and understanding.

INHERITANCE

———————◆———————

Legacies are a bone of contention for many grief-stricken families
— not just the obvious ones of money and possessions, but genes,
family status, beliefs, attitudes, culture and memories. When faced
with death and impermanence, we sometimes become agitated by
inheritance; but this is simply a distraction from the pain of loss.

WHEN PARENTS DIE, children often shoulder the
responsibility of deciding what to keep and what to
dispose of. Some belongings may be treasures that remind us
of our loved one, or perhaps of lost childhood; others feel like
a burden that we just want rid of. For some, possessions can
seem like a sacred trust that we can't bear to part with (even
though we may prefer to). Conversely, we might want to
make a clean sweep and get rid of everything in sight.
Nothing is clear-cut with grief. Strong feelings that affect one
family member won't apply to another.

When my own father died, the house was already packed
up ready for sale, so we felt that, initially, the safest place for
our distraught mother was the psychiatric hospital where she
was being treated for depression. When she then took her
own life twelve years later, we had to wash away the sadness
of her crushed paracetamol pills.[23] Both times, I was faced not
only with the trauma of their suicide and my own despair but
with the practical problem of clearing the house — neither of

which I was in a fit state to tackle. My brother and I attacked the house, literally, burning belongings, clearing out clothes – trying to impose order where there wasn't any.

Give It Time

I would always counsel allowing as much time as possible before making irreversible decisions following a death – but I know from first-hand experience that this is rarely feasible. We are usually too emotionally drained by bereavement to take sensible decisions of any note, yet the urgent business of day-to-day life carries on regardless. Even when traumatized and in a highly charged state, we are expected to make decisions. I regret very little in life – mindfulness teaches me the futility of wishing things were other than they are – but thirty years on, I still blanch at my knee-jerk reaction of sweeping away personal mementoes of my parents in a blind fury.

Clearing out a home, once the centre of family life, creates intense insecurity. We feel lonely and lost like an abandoned child, whatever age we are. This fear and anxiety feeds our desire to cling on to the past. Our stake in family property and possessions may come to represent our sense of well-being or where we belong on the ladder of our loved one's affections. The anger that rears its head when we are deprived of things we expect to inherit, can be a surprising feature of grief. Belongings, often all we're left with, become something we're ready to fight for even when there isn't the need.

Benediction

In many cultures, parents, when facing death, give their children a blessing — a sign of approval and trust. Western society no longer has such a symbolic benediction in its tradition but the sense and meaning of handing over the mantle from one generation to the next remains. 'Love' and 'approval' are important expressions for most of us, so when they are withheld we feel cheated and angry. On the other hand, when we feel valued and trusted, we blossom and flourish.

The Stuff of Dreams

Be cheerful, sir:
Our revels now are ended. These our actors,
As I foretold you, were all spirits and
Are melted into air, into thin air:
And, like the baseless fabric of this vision,
The cloud-capp'd towers, the gorgeous palaces.
The solemn temples, the green globe itself,
Yea, all which it inherit, shall dissolve
And, like this insubstantial pageant faded,
Leave not a rack behind. We are such stuff
As dreams are made on, and our little life
Is rounded with a sleep.

FROM 'THE TEMPEST'
WILLIAM SHAKESPEARE (PROSPERO, ACT IV, SCENE 1)

The Death of a Child

The death of a child is the most monstrously crushing, crippling and profound experience that any parent ever has to face. When a child dies before their parent, the natural order of life and death is turned on its head. The sensations of loss can be so intense that we feel possessed. No mother or father expects to be standing over their child's grave or scattering their ashes to the wind; parents are expected to love and protect their children and when a child dies, our grief feels unbearable.

Losing a child of any age – pre-term, baby, toddler, adolescent – creates a void inside that can never be filled, not completely. Sorrow permeates our soul. Recovering even the smallest glimmer of hope after such a mortifying event seems impossible for a very long time. The pain may last a lifetime. Children carry our genes, our DNA, into the future and when a child dies, all our hopes and dreams, vicariously imagined, are buried alongside. Part of us is lost forever.

A miscarriage or stillbirth, perhaps less visible to the outside world, is a birth requiring recognition and a death needing to be marked just like any other. My niece, a bereavement midwife in London, asks her community midwives, 'Would you leave your newborn baby with a stranger?' The answer is always 'no' and yet bereaved couples who lose a baby are expected to walk out of the hospital without their child.

One grieving mother carries a picture of her macerated stillborn baby inside a golden locket. For the unprepared it's a shocking revelation, whereas for the mother, she is simply cradling her beautiful little daughter lovingly to her heart. Another mother, when congratulated for a healthy delivery, sobbed, 'This isn't the baby I want, I want the one that died.'

A mother who loses her newborn baby is beyond pain. Yesterday she was pregnant, joyful, bursting with hope and anticipation, ready to celebrate new life – today she is being comforted, treated as though she's sick, questioned about mementoes and photographs of her dead child, locks of hair, post-mortems and funerals. Her grief and suffering is beyond endurance. Couples blame each other; siblings feel neglected and confused. IVF deaths can make the infertile parent feel guilty, the other angry and disappointed. Some couples even shoulder the burden of their parents' grief as well as their own. The emotional responses to the death of a child are earth-shattering, overwhelming and unpredictable.

SUZANNE'S STORY

SUZANNE's father committed suicide a short time after her younger stepsister from another marriage accused him of sexually abusing her. Another family member confirmed similar instances of molestation. My client believed the revelations – she was in no doubt. Paradoxically, her father had always been caring and protective towards her while growing up and the family had been fairly stable until her late adolescence, when he left. Suzanne maintained regular contact with him, although deep down she felt he never really cared much about her.

No charges of sexual abuse were made, although the police confirmed that this remained a possibility. A few days after the allegation was made, Suzanne's father killed himself. No suicide note was discovered but they found a carefully composed will in his car, close to the building from which he hurled himself.

The combination of her father's sudden and violent suicide and the shocking revelations of his sexual abuse left Suzanne consumed with rage. She was angry with her father for committing such terrible deeds; she raged against her mother for withdrawing emotionally; she was angry that she couldn't talk to her dead father and ask 'why?'; she was outraged that he had 'taken the coward's way out'; she was bitter about the shame, fear and grief that she felt and angry with her husband simply because he was there to berate. Her red-hot rage boiled over again and again during our sessions.

Anger is rather like taking a stick to oneself. We let rip with a tormented barrage of self-critical blows that leave us feeling battered, bruised, beaten – full of inadequacy, isolation and low self-esteem.

Sometimes, anger that is aimed at ourselves can be so vehement and unforgiving that it turns into suicide – or, as Sigmund Freud observed: Murder in the 180th degree.

Suzanne was literally a furnace of molten rage and during the twelve turbulent months since her father's death, had buried herself deeply into her children, work and home with unrelenting activity. She tried her best not to dwell on events but, every so often, the anger engulfed her and beat her to the ground, where she fell inconsolably.

The combination of her father's sudden and violent suicide and the shocking revelations of his sexual abuse left Suzanne consumed with rage.

Summary

Towards the end of our sessions, Suzanne wrote a moving testament to her dead father expressing her love and forgiveness. She accepted that she would never find answers but gave herself permission to welcome him back into her heart.

ANGER

JENNIFER'S STORY

JENNIFER and Jeremy married young. They enjoyed a stable, loving, spiritually satisfying relationship and reared five children who thrived and developed into gifted, fully rounded adults. Grandchildren arrived and both Jennifer and Jeremy flourished in their new role as grandparents.

The family was conventional in so far as both parents adopted traditionally defined roles. Jennifer had always been the warm, nourishing heart of the family and Jeremy the disciplined, entrepreneurial breadwinner. He worked hard to build up a successful business, providing his family with a comfortable home and his children with private education.

With retirement approaching, Jeremy decided to invest money into a plot of land in Corsica and build a beautiful holiday retreat. When the family wasn't using it, they could rent it out for additional income. Jennifer opposed the idea. At the very time when they were at last independent and free of debt, Jeremy insisted on borrowing money secured against their home. Having always been the provider, and a very good one, objections were confidently brushed aside and Jeremy had his way. His holiday home was realized.

Arriving home from a lovely family holiday in the villa, Jeremy unloaded the suitcases from the car and dropped down dead. No warning, no signs of illness, no indication that anything was wrong. He was sixty-four years of age. His death came in an instant and left the entire family devastated.

Jennifer was emotionally crushed. Her five children, themselves already devastated and grief-stricken, held her head lovingly above an ocean of grief, keeping her afloat. Then more disaster struck: the euro collapsed; income from tourism evaporated; interest rates soared. Jeremy's moneymaking dream in the sun became a financial nightmare for the grieving family.

Not only had Jennifer suffered the loss of Jeremy and all their shared hopes, she lost her financial security and was forced to sell the family home in order to repay high-interest borrowing on the house abroad – the one she had opposed. Jennifer was overwhelmed by both grief and misery, and yet also consumed with bitter rage towards her dead husband for leaving such a legacy.

Her five children, themselves
already devastated and grief-stricken,
held her head lovingly above an ocean
of grief, keeping her afloat.

Summary

Over time, I saw Jennifer's despair lessen and her resilience grow stronger. She occasionally berated Jeremy's stubborn arrogance but always with a smile and a forgiving heart. Death may have shattered their dreams but, for better or worse, their love continues.

5. **ONE STEP AT A TIME**

Walking reduces blood pressure and heart rate; creates feelings of well-being; helps manage stress, improves mood and encourages sleep. Walking, an activity available to most of us most of the time, not only brings obvious health benefits, but is a readily accessible method of focusing our attention on our natural rhythms. Walking can become an uplifting and soothing part of our daily life.[24]

When we place one foot in front of the other – mindfully, aware of what we are doing and paying full attention to the sights and sounds around us – we embrace the restorative rhythm of walking, anchoring ourselves to the present.

When you find your mind wandering off, come back to now. Walking is like a meditation; a way of moving without goal or intention, and of observing ourselves without self-criticism. It's all too easy to slip into an almost semi-conscious state of walking, where the legs are moving almost unaided but the mind is elsewhere.

This exercise is a step-by-step journey for reducing stress and enhancing your experience of everyday life.

1. Find your spot. Choose a place where you feel at ease, confident; it might be in the countryside, park, suburban street or back garden.

2. Find your senses. Bring your awareness to how you're standing, the feel of the ground beneath the soles of your feet, the texture, and your posture, how your legs are moving and the rhythm of your body. Notice how your body feels – is it heavy or light? Explore your sensations and allow time to notice the minute detail in everything.

3. Find your breath. Walk in silence, even when you're with somebody else; walk slowly, focusing on your breathing – inhale, exhale; count the number of steps to each breath. See how mindfulness heightens awareness of your surroundings.

6. **THE NATURAL WORLD**

We don't own the Earth; we share it with nature and every type of plant, wildlife and animal that embodies life. Although uniquely adaptable and triumphant as a species, we humans are just one of the many beautiful life-forms that inhabit the natural world.[25]

We have dominated and colonized virtually every ecosystem on Earth and our population growth surpasses all species on the planet; but if it weren't for the trees, the sun, the air that we breathe, we wouldn't exist. Waking up our senses inspires feelings of awe, connecting us to the universal cycle of birth, life and death. The sense of calmness that arises when we engage with the natural world will help us weather the storms of loss.

This exercise offers simple techniques for drawing on the healing peacefulness of nature.

1. Take a walk in a wood, park, or by the sea, to savour nature and soothe the mind. If you're with others, don't chatter; listen to the sounds around you, notice the flora and fauna. Stay attentive.

2. Find a pond, sit quietly, pay attention to the multitude of wildlife relishing the water; experience it through all your senses and really look, as though you are encountering everything for the very first time. Be aware of the breeze on your face, how your body feels; let go of the idea that you are separate — you are part of life.

3. Sit quietly in your own garden, experiencing nature every way you can; watch the clouds moving, the swooping swallows, notice the textures, hard and soft; allow yourself to feel infused with a sense of gentle calm. Be fully present to each moment.

Grief is a natural expression of human love; we will always sense the loss of our loved ones but by seeing ourselves as part of the natural world, we can enjoy being here.

CHAPTER THREE

BARGAINING

*Ten years ago I sat with Gerald, my
friend and art school mentor, as he struggled for air,
fighting his terror at the prospect of dying — which
sadly he did, two days later. I miss Gerald. I'm fortunate
to have some of his wonderful paintings adorning my
walls — like him, brushed full of vigour and life. Gerald
remains part of my inner and outer landscape. I wish his
death had been more peaceful — indeed, that he hadn't
died. I also wish he hadn't witnessed fear and
helplessness on my face that day, but mindfulness
teaches that we can't turn the clock back or
change past events. We must accept life,
as it is, without 'if only's.*

What is Bargaining?

Bargaining can be defined as negotiation — exchanging one thing for another in order to arrive at a happy settlement. The 'bargaining' over life and death that sometimes features during bereavement is a desperate attempt on our part to avoid the nightmare of loss.

To avoid the separating cuts of the Grim Reaper's scythe, we implore God, the doctor, the Devil, the hospice — anybody who will listen. Out of fear, feelings of injustice and sheer desperation, we will beg whoever or whatever we believe can influence the outcome. Our pleas come with an implicit promise that if only this one last single wish is granted, we will ask for or expect nothing more. Frantic for a reprieve, bargaining is our final attempt at exerting control over a situation in which we have none. There is no authority over dying, and death is beyond the reach of us all. Pleading for resurrection, absurd though it is, is our last-ditch bid at holding on to the person we love and cannot bear the thought of letting go.

Life is not owned; we all die. It's a hard fact of life.

The Remedy
The antidote to bargaining or pleading for the impossible is to recognize that we cannot turn the clock back or bring the

*Bargaining is our final attempt
at exerting control over a situation
in which we have none.*

dead back to life. Life is not owned; we all die. It's a hard fact
of life. Relief and recovery begin only when we accept that
death is an unavoidable truth of life. We must experience
what we are feeling, fully, here and now, acknowledge the
hard reality of our present situation, and be prepared to look
towards the future.

In the aftermath of death, we may dream of a reunion with
our loved one in a halcyon afterlife or be desperate to avoid
the pain of further tragedies. A parent grieving a dead child
might plead for the safety of their other children. We may try
to bargain that if nothing can be changed and our loved one
really can't be spared, then at least grant them a peaceful and
pain-free demise – please!

'Life can only be found in the present moment.
The past is gone, the future is not yet here, and if we do
not go back to ourselves in the present moment, we
cannot be in touch with life.'

FROM 'PEACE IS EVERY STEP'
THICH NHAT HANH, 1991 [26]

If Only...

When faced with death or terminal illness, we feel the panic rising inside and will do almost anything to avoid loss and postpone our pain. We bargain, we plead, we beg, we beseech. We try desperately to negotiate our way out of the terror of loss. 'I'll never be angry with my wife again if only you'll save her.' We make deals with our savage gods in a futile attempt to be spared the pain of separation. 'I'll give my life for hers.' 'I'll give my life savings if only...' We can't bear the pain of loss and long to be released from it – freed from the pain of life. We want our lives to be returned to normal, our loved one restored and life to be as it was.

The bargaining stage of bereavement is a futile expression of hope – hope that we can undo what has happened or at least circumnavigate the misery. If only, if only, if only... We become lost in an emotional maze, searching for ways out, alternative scenarios to the unfolding catastrophe. If only we had discovered the tumour sooner; if only I had recognized the symptoms earlier; if only we hadn't taken the car. We want the outcome to be different. We know that death is inevitable and yet we seek fruitless bargaining chips with which to negotiate a more bearable alternative.

We can't bear the pain
of loss and long to be released from it –
freed from the pain of life.

WHERE IS GOD?

When somebody we love dies, we feel in agony. For those with faith, God seems absent, to have deserted us. Where is God, we ask? Where was our watchful deity when I needed him/her/it the most? Why is he so damn cruel?

BELIEFS OFTEN DISAPPEAR INTO a bleak nothingness when a loved one dies. We question the meaning of life, of everything, and yet nothing has any meaning. We feel dead – zombie-like. Everything feels like a heavy black void and we see no beacon of light anywhere. We ask ourselves, if God is good then why does he make us suffer and hurt beyond our worst nightmares? God must be a depraved cosmic sadist that enjoys torturing us. Perhaps he's a lie, an invention and doesn't exist after all?

Do not mistake death for the Divine.[27] Death is not God. Instead, recognize death as an ever-present possibility in each moment of all our lives. Death comes calling when we least expect him, at any time, and can astonish us with his speed and cruelty. Death is neither chronological, charitable nor choosy. He is an ordinary, everyday, commonplace visitor who greets each one of us eventually.

Whatever doctrine we praise for the wonders of life gets shaken to its roots by death. When a loved one is taken away, our sanity vanishes along with them. Our mind totters precariously on a knife-edge and the hurt can be so intense that we would gladly give our soul to have them back again. We pray to have our precious one restored, even when we claim no faith, and we beg that somebody, anybody, will answer our prayers. Unfortunately, all our bargaining and pleas are futile and fall on deaf ears. Our loved one is gone. Death is indisputable and irreversible; nothing can bring them back and we must accept it.

Faith & Bereavement

In writing a book about bereavement, it is impossible to avoid the 'God question' because God and bereavement are intrinsically linked in so many people's minds. I lay my cards on the table at this point and confess to being an agnostic. I can't believe in the existence of a creator, I've tried; so in that sense I have no formal religious faith. And yet I do. I believe in the natural order of the universe and that there is something of God in us all. I believe we are personally responsible for being good and bad – not a higher authority, not a deity – and I try to value everybody equally. I have my own moral compass that I do my best to follow but, like most of us, I often fall short of my destination.

In terms of a divine faith, I have none. My own creed welcomes occasional silence and quiet thoughtfulness as a restorative antidote to busyness. My personal mindfulness clinic is a run on the Sussex Downs, walking by the sea, yoga, time spent working in the garden or the occasional ritual of a Quaker meeting, where silence is the shared medicine. I have come to realize that quietness pulls me back to the present moment from which I always seem to be running. Quiet time helps me reflect on my work as a publisher, my family, my friendships, my voluntary work and my day-to-day life.

When my mother killed herself all those years ago, twelve years after my father's suicide, my head and heart were full of rage, sadness and regret. I felt I would never fully recover or be free of those feelings. I remember ranting to my dead mother while running on the Downs and having tearful con- versations, telling her how much I loved her and asking her the deafening question of why? Why? There was no answer, just a roaring silence. It was a time of madness during which I felt haunted and cursed by both my parents.

The Quest for Meaning

In the course of my bereavement work, God and Christianity often enter the room alongside my clients. As indeed do Spiritualism, Buddhism, Hinduism, Agnosticism, Islamism, Judaism, Realism – all the 'isms' have come into sessions at some point. Following a death, the quest for meaning is inten- sified and is often fundamental to our journey through grief. Beliefs, doubts, questions: we interrogate our psyches and death shines a spotlight on our search. Why are we here? What is the point? Why must we be parted from those we love?

For Those Bereaved by Suicide

Death by suicide makes loss particularly unbearable because suicide is so often accompanied by shame, stigma, prejudice and shock. Depression, often the culprit of suicide but a commonplace ailment like many others, is judged by some to imply madness, neurosis and failure. Self-murder is still a taboo subject: one that people avoid out of fear and embarrassment. Until recently, suicide remained a crime that even the Church judged morally insane, judging the perpetrator unworthy of heavenly sanctuary.

The act of suicide cuts across all sexes, ages and economic barriers. Rich and poor, men and women, young children, old people and adolescents all take their lives. Nobody is immune to self-inflicted death. Why anyone would willingly extinguish their life remains a conundrum of the human condition – hopelessness; anguish; depression; despair; intense pain? Perhaps those who end their lives are not choosing death so much as seeking an end to the unbearable suffering that they're experiencing?

Some believe that everyone has the right to end their life; others think suicide is a sin or an act of cowardice. Whatever our stance, the impact of suicide on those left behind is lifelong. When a loved one dies it is devastating: when a loved one dies by their own hand, the grief, already terrible, is magnified by feelings of disgrace, incomprehension, confusion and rage. Survivors of suicide often feel responsible, guilty, angry, isolated, confused and abandoned. Corrosive thoughts such as these may be further compounded by social inhibition and stigma. The ripples of suicide touching the lives of those left behind are overpowering and far-reaching.

Although there is no hierarchy of grief where death is concerned, there is no doubt that suicide is particularly harrowing. The unanswerable question of *why* a loved one kills themselves usually remains an open wound, weeping forever. The whirlpool of suicide leaves deep and permanent scars. 'Could I have done something to prevent their death?' 'Was I responsible?' Why, why, why? The person who knows the answer isn't there to enlighten, let alone reassure us; all we can do is accept that their misery was so great, killing themselves felt like the best choice – their last resort.

Mindfulness teaches us to enter into each moment completely, neither distorting the past nor hiding from the future. To accept a death by suicide and open our hearts to compassion and forgiveness is an opportunity for us to make peace with our lost one as well as with our own torment.

Why do we suffer? These are philosophical conundrums to which we must find our own answers. Everyone has the right to seek their own truth but we must respect and tolerate each other, no matter which path we choose to follow.

When I'm counselling, I remain neutral about faith. The client/counsellor relationship is such that there are strict boundaries in which to work. Ethically, I have a duty to remain objective and encourage clients towards beneficial outcomes. I support independent freethinking and their right to make whatever decisions they choose. The work is always about *their* beliefs, *their* feelings, and *their* decisions, not mine. I balance establishing firm boundaries with making warm, empathetic relationships in which clients trust me with their despair and innermost vulnerabilities. Although I'm there as a touchstone for somebody else's feelings, it's not unusual to be asked questions about aspects of my own life – including whether or not I believe in God.

I always turn the question back on itself and encourage my clients to talk about what they believe in. God is a personal concept. We see the creative force of the world everywhere around us but we experience it through our own eyes. Whether devout or secular, born-again or objective realist, the meaning of life is a treasure we all seek. If an individual's philosophy brings comfort and bolsters up their spirits, I consider that to be beneficial. We must each discover our own truth, and our own reasons for getting out of bed to face the day.

NOT JUST FOR BUDDHISTS

◆

Mindfulness may originate from ancient Buddhist beginnings but it is a recipe for healthy living available to everyone in today's world. Finding peace and fulfilment in the present, not the past or future, allows us to savour the satisfying taste of authentic contentment.

MINDFUL PRACTICE DOESN'T PRECLUDE a divine belief, it simply places responsibility for our thoughts, feelings and actions firmly in our own hands. Happiness is not something ready-made – it comes from our own efforts and actions. If we evaluate mindfulness in this way, focus on the here-and-now and look to ourselves for solutions, not to others, we will find grief cathartic and our present realities more tolerable.

The death of somebody we love brings monumental change into our life but it is still an ordinary, everyday experience that we share with every person that ever drew breath. We arrive in this world and we leave. The mindful appreciation of all the moments in between, and the realization that joy and sorrow are not mutually exclusive but coexist side by side, is intrinsic to a fulfilling journey. The river of life in which we all swim is a divine miracle. The memory of my loved ones flowing into me and I, in turn, flowing into the lives of all the people who love me, is a powerful metaphor – for we are all participants in the stream of memory that surges through humanity and binds us together. We can embrace these thoughts and still, should we choose, allow space in our lives for the Divine.

Seeking Truth

As the practice of mindfulness stems from Buddhist roots, I asked a lifelong friend and Buddhist teacher, Ngak'chang Rinpoche, to give me his explanation for how God and Buddhism might coexist in the twenty-first century and he replied:

'I have friends of other religions and we speak of our similarities rather than our differences. This is simple for me because Buddhism is a *religion of method* rather than a *religion of truth*, and therefore sees other religions in the same light.

Method points to truth and each of us requires different methods to discover truth: so there is no problem when methods appear to contradict each other. Buddhism is atheistic (having no God) but that does not mean I must argue with God as a method for seeking truth. Many are suited to this approach. The point of view that different religions are simply different methods for seeking truth is one that allows not only tolerance – but also appreciation of the rich variety of ways that can illuminate our understanding of creation and the human condition.

Different religions are simply different methods for seeking truth.

Buddhism does not have a God as the creator.

Some say 'Emptiness is another way of describing God.' While I could not agree with that idea, I do respect it.

Everyone has to make sense of other religions in their own way. Every religion will have its own way of viewing other religions — and as long as there is real appreciative-openness to the value of other religions, no one need argue.

Discovery Through Experience

Every method — being *method* rather than *the truth to which it points* — will have drawbacks with regard to understanding the human situation. The conundrum with Buddhist atheism is that it may be interpreted by some as nihilism because Buddhism does not have a God as the creator. Buddhism does not require belief in anything: everything has to be discovered through experience. Nihilism, however, is not the Buddhist experience of religion.

The self-creating nature of the universe is experienced as a treasury of endless marvels — and the moment-by-moment birth and death of existence is a manifestation of that incredible wealth. If we accept birth and death as the texture of an authentic experience of life — embracing both sorrow and joy — we can never feel that reality has been unjust, or that anything should be other than it is.'

PATRICK'S STORY

PATRICK was in his mid-sixties. Maureen, his wife, had been dead for a year when he came to the drop-in. She had been rushed into hospital following a minor stroke, which led to respiratory problems and then death. Patrick's doctor prescribed antidepressants but he wouldn't take them, adamant he wasn't depressed. He said he was grieving and that nothing would or ever could change how he felt. When Patrick refused to see a psychiatrist, his doctor suggested the group.

Patrick was convinced that Maureen's life had been taken unnecessarily — caused by medical negligence. He instigated a formal complaint procedure that was being investigated by the hospital trust. He raged at the hospital, the nurses and most of all, the uncaring consultant who had let his wife die. They had killed her. He was convinced the hospital was covering its tracks and was determined to get answers.

Patrick and Maureen had been together since teenagers: without her, he was completely lost. He had never had to cook a meal, worry about money, tend the garden or pay a bill. Maureen did everything. They never had children but they had each other and that had been more than enough. He said they were always blissfully happy and that he had never wanted anyone or anything else.

When Patrick wasn't berating the hospital for its criminal care, he was crying inconsolably and saying how much he wanted to join Maureen. When we digged deeper and I asked him whether he ever experienced suicidal thoughts, it transpired that Patrick went to her grave every day. However, Maureen was buried sixty miles away, next to his parents, and as he didn't drive, that meant an hour's train journey and then a taxi – two hours each way. Come rain or shine, Patrick would embark on his daily pilgrimage and spend the entire daylight hours sitting there talking to her, weeping and tending her plot. It was winter so the days were short, but he was yearning for the long summer evenings when they could spend even more time together.

There were many 'if only's and misery beyond description; but when asked whether Maureen would want him to spend all day every day at the cemetery, Patrick was in no doubt. 'Yes, I know that's what she would want because that's what she would do for me.' Patrick literally wanted to climb down into the grave with her – he had tried to do so at her funeral; but if he couldn't do that then NOTHING would convince him to stop his vigil or reduce his visits.

He pleaded and begged that he would give anything to have Maureen back – anything. Although he acknowledged she wasn't coming back, Patrick felt sure it wouldn't be long before he joined her and they would be together again. And in the meantime, well, he had the battle with the hospital to absorb him, which, if victorious, would somehow restore Maureen back to him.

Summary

Patrick eventually saw a psychiatrist while continuing our sessions. He became angry with friends for encouraging him to spend less time at the cemetery, but he gradually picked up the threads of a more balanced life: volunteering at a local primary school, enjoying the fellowship of friends, visiting Maureen's grave and looking forwards.

ANNA'S STORY

ANNA's sixteen-year-old daughter, Jessie, had killed herself in her bedroom twelve months earlier. Always a troubled teenager, though close to her mother, Jessie had gone quietly upstairs one evening on the pretext of watching television and strangled herself into unconsciousness. She had strapped her neck to the bedstead with a belt, and then using her own body weight, had acted as her own executioner. Jessie had literally pulled the life breath out of her own squirming body.

Her thirteen-year-old brother Jason had gone upstairs to find his sister choking to death, and after a nightmare few minutes of hysteria and terror, Anna had called the emergency services. Mother and son, already deeply traumatized, suffered five more days of unbearable torture while the hospital fought valiantly, but in vain, to restore Jessie's life.

Jessie's parents had divorced years earlier. Her father was an unreliable alcoholic, though he kept in touch. But there was little love lost between the extended family members and it seemed there was always tension of one sort or another. The police had removed intimate diaries revealing Jessie's ongoing battles with self-harm, bullying, a friend's death and her own feelings of worthlessness – all of which were well disguised in the various photographs on display. They misleadingly showed a beautiful, vibrant young woman, with everything ahead of her, at the centre of school parties and nights out with friends, seemingly without a care in the world.

The police liaison officer was kind and supportive but Anna still had to endure the torment of a painful inquest, aggressive relations and the increasingly disruptive behaviour of her son Jason. No wonder my client just wanted to go to sleep and never wake up! She was struggling to survive and find a way through her grief and back to life.

Anna would have exchanged her own life for that of her daughter without a second thought. She would have given anything to hear her laughter again or go shopping together; but, instead, Anna was sentenced to a life of continuous self-flagellation. She kept Jessie's room as a shrine, spending long hours there searching for relief and trying to resuscitate her daughter's spirit. If only she hadn't left her alone in her bedroom? If only she had been able to save her? If only she had been a better mother? Whatever bargains she tried to make with herself, there was no way back to life as it had been before the terrible tragedy.

> *There was no way back*
> *to life as it had been before*
> *the terrible tragedy.*

Summary
There was no sudden change or miracle cure, but a gradual shift. Jason started counselling sessions with a colleague and Anna returned to work. Mother and son stayed close, fearful of letting the other out of sight. Survivors of their own holocaust, I know from experience that their particular journey will take a lifetime to travel.

7. **LOSS OF INTIMACY**

Displaying passion for somebody we love through touch and sexual intimacy is a normal human desire. Most of us yearn to hold, be held, and to enjoy the bonding experience of erotic pleasure. When we lose an intimate partner, we feel robbed of human touch and sexual expression. Sexual energy is a primal force in most lives and masturbation – responding to the normal workings of our bodies and hormones – is nothing to feel ashamed or embarrassed about.

Responding to, embracing and accepting our needs is treating ourselves tenderly and with love. At first, we may find it impossible to imagine being with somebody else, or see a new relationship as betrayal; but we can't restore the dead and we still have the right to life, companionship and happiness. How can we find healthy, safe, achievable outlets for touch in our early stages of grief?

1. A visit to the hairdresser or a gentle aromatherapy massage can make us feel comforted, stroked, soothed, and physically alive.

2. Relaxing in a hot bath or sauna calms and reduces stress; and bathing by candlelight creates an ambience of nurturing kindness.

3. Self-massage or Shiatsu – finger pressure – helps put us back in touch with our sexual energy. Practising Shiatsu with a trusted friend is healing, stimulating and fun.

4. Sharing a bed for companionship works for some, but if you're turning to a fuck buddy for comfort, do take care and look after yourself, both physically and emotionally.

5. Online sex, although easily available, is anonymous, damaging and unconcerned with equality or love. Falling into such encounters out of insecurity, loneliness or frustration, while tempting, won't bring happiness – but living mindfully pulls us towards trusting, tender, loving and compassionate relationships.

8. PETS

Nothing can replace a loved one in our hearts but keeping a domestic pet can provide a real boost to our emotional well-being during the struggle with grief. Pets depend on us to care for, feed and cuddle them, and in return they show warmth and affection. Their unconditional love and empathy is profoundly healing. Stroking a pet lowers blood pressure, soothes our worried minds, and increases the levels of naturally occurring feel-good chemicals – serotonin and dopamine – that help us resist depression.

Pets give us something to care for, something outside of ourselves to think about, companionship, the sense of living with another being; they foster social contact, help overcome loneliness and feelings of isolation, encourage interaction with nature – in itself therapeutic – and create feelings of security. Pets provide us with many positive gifts, not least because they live firmly in the present, instinctive and sentient. They don't premeditate, plan ahead, dwell in the past or future; they are very accepting, curious, living for whatever is happing in the moment.

Here are some exercises where indulgent joy with your pet might help you become happier, more balanced.

1. Exercise: play with your pet, connect, listen, pay attention, be in the moment with them; if you have a dog, go for plenty of walks – you'll feel happier, healthier, and so will your faithful companion.

2. Touch: animals don't care about words – they recognize what's going on intuitively, responding to body language, being stroked; they need time and attention, encouraging our nurturing side.

3. Talking: dogs provide lots of opportunities for social interaction. I know two recently bereaved dog owners whose dogs (same breed) have fallen in love with each other – as have the dog owners.

CHAPTER FOUR

DEPRESSION

*I've never been crippled by depression,
not yet; but this cruel, melancholic killer
overcame both my parents and has since
blighted the lives of several close friends. The
condition of depression, not sorrow or sadness, is an
invisible hooligan waiting to pull us down into a dark
abyss of grief and despair. Mindfulness invites us to 'be
with' the dreadful experience – seeing our situation
clearly, helping us choose the best ways to respond.
When mourning the loss of a loved one, it is
natural to feel a deep sense of grief – but
this need not become depression.*

THE DEPTHS OF DESPAIR

◆

Depression affects both mind and body, making us feel physically leaden and psychologically helpless. Although one of the brutal consequences of loss — when sadness overwhelms us as the reality of our situation kicks in — depression can also signify the prelude to acceptance. Hurrah!

THE DEPRESSIVE STAGE OF GRIEF can feel as though it will last forever. We become trapped in a black hole of hopelessness and nothingness. 'I miss my loved one so much, why go on?' 'What's the point, I'm going to die soon anyway.' The idea of living, coping, carrying on, can seem utterly pointless. We feel our heart is broken, never to be mended; we focus on past happiness, regret, guilt for things said or done and lost opportunities.

Following on the heels of pointless pleading, trying to alter things we cannot change, our attention shifts to the present as we begin to understand the finality of death. We feel weighed down by our fear of the future and our longing for the past. In depression, we become caught in ever depleting spirals of despair, unable to see any way out. Things lose all meaning and grief enters us at a deeper level than we might ever have imagined possible. The weight of loss settles stubbornly into our souls as we realize our loved one has gone forever and is never coming back.

The Remedy

The antidote to depression is hope and gratitude. Hope that tomorrow may be better and gratitude for what we have.

When depressed, we become silent and morose; we may withdraw, refuse to see people and disconnect from friends and family; we might spend much of our time crying inconsolably but not want, or know how, to talk about it; we might feel so tired and poleaxed by grief that we just want to stay in our bed; we may feel heavy and lethargic and lose our appetite. When we're on our own, we want company and when we have it, we want to be alone. Dreams can be disturbing and we constantly yearn for the thing we want most but can never regain. There is an invisible veil of despair surrounding us that separates us from the rest of the world. Life has changed permanently and will never be as it was.

Loss makes us feel as though a door has been slammed shut on a deep attachment forever but, in time, we will gradually see another door opening – one that leads to the rest of our lives. To deny sorrow or the importance of loss is to deny

---

'Hope is important because it can make the
present moment less difficult to bear. If we believe that
tomorrow will be better, we can bear a hardship today.'

FROM 'PEACE IS EVERY STEP'
THICH NHAT HANH, 1991

---

loving because love is the fuel driving grief. The trek through bereavement can eventually lead to profound insight that reaches beyond individual loss – but this takes time to achieve. The intense pain of loss is only temporary; it passes eventually. Mindfulness can help us bear the pain of our journey. Grieving mindfully is a process of gently putting the pieces of ourselves back together again, consciously, fully appreciating what we have lost and giving us insight into who we are.

Murderous Melancholia

During the depressed stage it may be that all we can do is sit and do nothing except think about the person who has gone – but this sitting, doing nothing, is in fact part of attaining acceptance. Feelings of sadness, regret and fear are natural; but if our depression continues to deepen and thoughts of suicide enter our minds, we must seek help quickly.

We may not want to share suicidal thoughts or know how to. They might feel too complex, too confusing – a secret. We may think dark thoughts but feel convinced we won't act them out. Conversely, suicide may seem so inevitable that we have already devised our plan. Paradoxically, talking about these feelings, however hard, can be a positive step towards acceptance and recovery. It is important that we take care of ourselves and one of the most therapeutic things we can do during bereavement is to talk about the person who has died and our relationship with them.

We should try not to isolate ourselves or judge ourselves weak for needing help. We may seek release in alcohol or drugs but such relief will only be temporary and, most likely, impede our recovery. We must tell people what we need and ask for help. There is nothing to be gained from suffering in silence. Talk to your doctor; call the Samaritans;[28] speak to a friend. We mustn't allow our melancholia to murder us.

MINDFULNESS VERSUS MEDICATION

Paradoxically, for many, the experience of death brings new meaning and spiritual growth. Death helps us to realise that everything around us is in a state of continual flux and that nothing in life is guaranteed or permanent.

DEATH OFFERS US AN OPPORTUNITY to pause and look at the deeper questions in our lives; to find purpose. We come to appreciate that genuine reality is to be found in the full appreciation of the present moment. Of course we feel sad and distressed when a loved one dies and our life is forever changed but grief is not an illness. Bereavement is a natural process to face, accept and work through – not a disease to treat or hide from.

Mostly, we are neither crippled nor incapacitated by grief. Given the remedy of time, comfort and support from friends and family, most of us are able to overcome the death of a loved one and reconstruct meaningful lives for ourselves. Although extremely challenging, we can all learn to accept the altered state that death brings and make the necessary adjustments to move forwards. Step by step, the majority of us can travel through the stages of grief towards recovery naturally, successfully and without medical treatment or intervention.

Mindfulness is an increasingly popular tool for calming the mind and soothing our emotional well-being, with passionate advocates internationally and within the British Parliament and National Health Service. Mindfulness can be a transformational tool when struggling with loss and depression but we have to put in the work and commit to the practice.

Beyond Grief

For some, however, bereavement can grow into an illness. We become devoured by corrosive emotions such as guilt, blame or anger and lapse into the malady of clinical depression. We begin to feel that life is no longer worth living; we lose our appetite and have difficulty in sleeping; we feel lethargic and psychologically blunted; we become sluggish and stop feeling the ordinary pleasures and sorrows of life. It can be very difficult distinguishing between grief and depression because many of the manifestations of depression are similar to those of bereavement. But if we feel we're not coping and the lines between sadness and sickness are becoming blurred, we must seek medical help.

Depression is a commonplace ailment found in people of all ages. It can strike anybody, however robust. Statistics determine that one in four of us will experience some kind of mental health problem during the course of any one year.[29] Anxiety and depression are often invisible to those around us because we try our best to put on a brave face. On the outside we can appear as normal – no visible plaster casts or bandages – but inside, we hurt like hell. Depression sucks our energy dry and crushes all motivation. Feelings of hopelessness, worthlessness and failure drive us deeper and deeper into a fog of despair through which we can see no glint of daylight.

It is worth noting that depression is usually about the past, about things that have happened, while anxiety is concern for the future, what may lie ahead. Let the present moment be free of both emotions, if possible, because both are fruitless.

Making Life Tolerable

The word 'antidepressant' strikes fear into many people but for some, antidepressant medication can help to manage the difficult journey of bereavement. Prescribed properly and monitored with care, antidepressants are neither addictive nor do they give an artificial high. There should be no shame in choosing any treatment that relieves anxiety and lifts our mood during a time of crisis.

There are now many different types of medication to choose from. It may take time to find the one that suits us best but if used correctly, under proper supervision from a doctor or mental health professional, antidepressants can take the edge off depression just enough to make life tolerable. Antidepressant medication, when prescribed responsibly and diligently, helps many of us allay the debilitating effects of anxiety and depression.

In 2013, antidepressants were prescribed fifty-three million times by National Health Service professionals in the UK. This sounds like an epidemic and indeed we should tread carefully. Over-prescribed and unmonitored use can present serious risks. During my mother's struggle with depression, which she unfortunately lost, she ended up with enough prescribed medication in the house to kill an army. In her despair, they became an all too readily available lethal weapon. We should always keep our doctor informed of how we're feeling, changes in mood or plans for reducing our dosage.

Mindful practice and talking therapies are more natural alternatives to medication but we each have to choose our preferred remedy. Each one of us has to confront bereavement eventually and accept the difficult experience of loss. There are no alternatives, no short cuts and no way of avoiding the true nature of our feelings. In order to heal we must accept the hard reality that somebody we love is dead and gone. We must fully experience our journey of suffering. Mindfulness enables us to walk through our grief. It empowers us to relate honestly with whatever arises, as it arises.

Bereavement Journals

The pain suffered after a death can be likened to a bewildering and life-shattering storm in which it's easy to feel lost and disorientated. Experiencing and recording our feelings, day by day, in the moment, is a powerful way of navigating and charting our headway through the fog of bereavement.

Grief is a temporary madness: our minds are confused, our lives disrupted. It feels impossible to hold the tiller steady or see the way ahead clearly. But we must face forwards, embrace the storm head on or we will sink. Rather than drowning in despair, we can record our feelings and moods in a bereavement journal. A diary for the soul: a safe and secure way of identifying the highs and lows of our emotional turbulence as we move back and forwards through grief.

We must allow ourselves to ride out the storm – not fight or oppress it. Even the darkest storm doesn't last forever. While we are being thrown about by turbulent waves of loss we must remember that our breath is our anchor, our wheel and our rudder. Keep focused on the breath.

When we review our journal, armed with a keener sense of awareness, we will see that even in the midst of suffering and confusion, we have been able to express celebration, generosity, hope and healing. We will notice small signs of recovery but it takes time and we must be patient.

ELSIE'S STORY

ELSIE's husband Tom committed suicide when she was fifty-three. They had lived a turbulent and sometimes violent marriage together and she divorced him for his gambling, drinking and womanizing in her late twenties. They remarried less than a year later. He could be very charming and persuasive when he chose to be and, thereafter, they were bound together in a destructive, co-dependent and damaging relationship made up of romantic love, explosive arguments and simmering frustration.

Despite being neurotic, Elsie was a loving, hard-working and devoted mother, while Tom was a brooding, bullying, unpredictable and sometimes unstable father. However, despite this emotionally perilous and dysfunctional environment, they raised three sons somewhat better than anybody might have predicted.

When he was thirty, Tom suffered his first epileptic seizure and this, together with other health problems, gradually took its toll. When he was forty-eight he became depressed and took an overdose. Although Tom survived this first suicide attempt, he felt ashamed, consumed by rage – which he fired directly at the son who rescued him.

Things slowly returned to a reproachful normality and remained that way for a further decade. When their youngest son left home for college, the fragile stability finally collapsed and Tom took his own life. He was sixty years old.

Like her dead husband, Elsie suffered bouts of crippling black-dog depression. When Tom killed himself she was overwhelmed with feelings of anger, guilt, abandonment, despair and loneliness from which she never recovered. She tried repeatedly to pick up her life – irrevocably damaged by past events – but she was ill-equipped emotionally and didn't have the resilience to survive her monumental tragedies. Each time she tried to stand up she fell back down again.

In between periods of deep depression she moved house several times in failed attempts to move her life forwards. Finally, trapped in a house with her matriarchal and overbearing mother (who was herself unable to cool her fury towards her dead son-in-law), Elsie plummeted downwards in a spiral of despair and depression. She was overwhelmed. Her three sons did their best to support her but they too were suffering from a lifetime of family trauma and in the end, despite trying, they couldn't change events or stop their mother sinking into the abyss.

During a particularly dangerous and disruptive episode of depression that hurled the family ever deeper into chaos and catastrophe, Elsie – by now living alone – stopped her addictive antidepressant medication and took a large overdose of paracetamol. The tablets didn't kill her outright – they left her with fatal liver damage from which she died a few days later. Tragedy and depression had triumphed.

Summary

Although Elsie didn't survive her grief, Elsie and Tom's three sons did. They flourished, both professionally and in their relationships. Despite traumatic childhoods, they all turned forwards and faced their lives bravely – with feelings of compassion and understanding towards their dead parents.

ALISON'S STORY

ALISON's daughter Lucy was a bright, energetic, passionate girl of eight who suffered asthma attacks. Since first being diagnosed at three, Lucy and her mother had participated in clinical tests at their local ear, nose and throat hospital. Lucy went for monthly check-ups with her consultant and had regular allergy tests; but other than that, she was a normal, happy, beautiful, clever girl who played football and loved her mum.

One morning, Lucy wolfed down a bowl of breakfast cereal that Alison had given her and almost immediately collapsed onto the floor, fitting. Paramedics were on the scene within minutes but by that time Lucy had turned blue and stopped breathing.

Lucy was rushed by ambulance to the local hospital and she was then transferred to London. After three days of emotional annihilation, Alison agreed to her life support being switched off. The pain, loss and the ordeal were unbearable.

Lucy had suffered a fatal allergic reaction to a new cereal. No one knew she had developed the allergy. Everybody assumed she was having an asthma attack – not going into cardiac arrest.

Alison showed me plaster casts of Lucy's handprints and footprints and photographs taken at her deathbed – her little pale body shrouded in swathes of tubes and medical paraphernalia. When I looked at a picture of her, suspended between life and death, it was impossible to hold back my own tears. It was the first time since Lucy's death three months earlier that Alison had been able to look at these pictures. She was inconsolable.

Alison described her rising panic whenever she went into the kitchen where Lucy collapsed and she still couldn't go into her bedroom. She often felt suicidal. As a mother, she felt she should have protected her – not fed her poison. She lived near the churchyard where her daughter was buried. Some days she would walk trance-like across the fields and lie on the ground next to her – rocking back and forth, trying to reclaim what was lost.

The effect on the family, her other children and herself was devastating. Lucy's father was back at work and wanted to move on. The family was fracturing. The consultant at the hospital encouraged Alison to talk with other bereaved parents but her husband resisted. How would that help? He wanted life to be normal.

Alison tried to block out her dark and despairing thoughts but panic gripped her throat – choking down her will to go on. Her depression deepened and every day was filled with torment, blame and guilt.

As a mother, she felt she should have protected her – not fed her poison.

Summary

Alison fought valiantly for her life, which she is gradually rebuilding. She established a charitable trust in honour of her daughter Lucy, raising money to support research into childhood asthma and other fatal allergies.

9. **SOWING THE SEEDS OF A NEW BEGINNING**

There is something magical about germination. You plant a seed, feed, water, pay attention to it, watch new growth struggle through the soil towards daylight – and then all your hard work blossoms into the gardener's gold of nature's bounty.

Nurturing gardens cultivate qualities we require for mindful living: acceptance, observation, patience, trust in ourselves and nature – allowing things to grow in their own time, accepting the harvest as it comes and letting go of expectation, being benevolent throughout the seasons, celebrating the fruits of our labour.

Gardening is a wonderful outlet for depression, anxiety and stress – it is restorative and rewarding, pulling us back into the present moment. The journey through loss and the cycle of gardening share many things: both are organic, natural processes, happening everywhere, every day. In gardening, as in loss, we must pay attention to what we plant, get the timing right, work hard, focus on conditions and then, hey presto – magic happens.

1. Pay attention to the soil; we must accept the raw base that nature provides but wise gardeners do everything they can to create optimum conditions for their seeds to flourish.

2. Observe your garden; sit, breathe, watch; appreciate the smells and texture of nature's miracles.

3. Notice your weeds but remember, weeds are only weeds when they overwhelm and strangle everything else. Sometimes, what others identify as bad, corrupt, ugly, are in fact wonderful, beautiful plants that should be cherished alongside their companions.

Gardening is the cycle of life – never to be tamed or completely controlled but appreciated and accepted all the same, for both its joys and its disappointments.

10. **THE POWER OF FORGIVENESS**

When Nelson Mandela, human rights lawyer and freedom fighter, walked out of prison in 1990 after serving twenty-seven years for resisting the brutal, white supremacy system of apartheid in South Africa, he freed himself and his nation from chains of suffering by his act of forgiveness.

Mindfulness teaches us to release the burden of hateful, angry feelings and be forgiving. When we suffer perceived hurt at the hands of somebody else, we lock ourselves into a prison of resentment, fear and loathing. We try to protect ourselves because we dread our own vulnerability. We even hold grudges towards people who are dead, in the deluded belief that somehow we can still make them suffer. We want them to pay for what they've done to us. But why continue our torture by holding on to ill feelings and an unwillingness to pardon? We should embrace the healing wisdom of forgiveness and honour the principle 'Do no harm'.

Forgiveness cannot be forced but the following exercise may help release the strain of past anger and anguish so you can touch the present moment with kindness and an open heart.

1. Allow yourself to remember and visualize the source of your own grudges. Why do you feel so hurt and betrayed? Why do you feel so much anger and pain? Picture each painful memory and every hateful perpetrator.

2. Try to imagine the hurt that you've caused by your aggression or thoughtless actions towards yourself and others. Remind yourself of your own angry words and toxic thoughts.

3. Be forgiving of yourself and accepting of others. Let go of anger and allow yourself the generosity of forgiveness. Be kind to yourself and to others, and allow yourself to heal.

CHAPTER FIVE

ACCEPTANCE

*Twenty years ago, two close friends lost their
first child, Martha, at eighteen months to a rare
genetic malformation. She is buried in my downland
garden in a simple plot marked by flints and wild
flowers. I felt their grief vicariously but sadly, apart
from being supportive, there was little I could do. I'm
sure they thrashed and screamed but they were also
thankful for Martha's short life – accepting,
surrendering to the situation. Bolstered by their
religious faith, each other and a determination to
live, my friends survived. They now have two other
lovely children but Martha remains their firstborn,
never to be replaced, always loved and still
part of their family.*

ARRIVING AT ACCEPTANCE

◆

Acceptance is receiving the reality of a situation. It is recognizing something without feeling the need to try and change it. It is taking a gift when offered, positively, not reluctantly. It is ceasing the urge to resist — surrendering to reality.

To RECOVER OURSELVES AFTER A DEATH we must make room for distressing feelings – allowing them to come and go without a struggle. We shouldn't fight grief but rather open ourselves up to reality, however painful. Cry whenever we feel the need to cry. During our exhausting trudge through bereavement, we must accept the unchangeable: the person we love and desire is dead and no longer with us in a physical sense. When we embrace this difficult reality alongside our feelings of sadness and loss, letting these emotions dance together, we become calmer and can begin the task of reconstructing meaning in our lives.

Grieving mindfully means allowing our emotional vulnerabilities to come out, redirecting our pain and distress into our personal growth as a human being. To move forwards, we must invest emotional energy into new social interactions, without guilt or self-criticism. Passing through this final stage of grief into acceptance is a long, precarious journey that mindful practice will help us navigate. We desperately want to feel whole again, yet we know that part of us is missing.

We will always feel a sense of loss but we must turn bravely forwards and face the reality of our changed situation.

The Remedy

Although we don't want to prolong grief, sometimes we feel unable to gather the strength required to pull ourselves up. We become stuck and can move neither forwards nor backwards. Life is changed forever; we know this: it can never be as it was before our bereavement. We must embrace this truth, acknowledge the finality of our loss and absorb the hard realities of our new situation. We must understand and accept the changes, adjust to the new dynamics of where we find ourselves and go forwards with our life. Awareness is allowing ourselves to accept the pain of loss.

Death makes us feel threatened and helpless but we can learn to observe these feelings, acknowledge them without self-judgement and let them go. We will always feel sad about losing a loved one but by cultivating mindfulness, we make room for new ways of observing our sorrow, becoming both more aware and more pragmatic. We must try not to indulge

---

'For after all, the best thing one can do

when it is raining is to let it rain.'

FROM 'TALES OF A WAYSIDE INN'
HENRY WADSWORTH LONGFELLOW, 1863 [30]

---

our sadness or be at the mercy of self-destructive emotions. Suffering feeds on suffering.

The Insane Ape

In Tibetan (Vajrayana) Buddhism, there is an analogy of being ridden by one's emotions. It describes 'having an insane ape on our back'. This insane ape (our emotions) forces a cold, ruthless bit between our teeth, jerking, pulling us back, our mouths bleeding. At the same time the ape wears razor-sharp spurs that are employed with gusto, raking our flanks, driving us on. The more we thrash and scream, the more satisfaction the insane ape feels.

We can allow ourselves to be sad and embrace our sorrow but we mustn't allow the insane ape to ride on our backs or become our friend. During the agonizing struggle that occurs after a loved one dies, we become caught in a spiral of emotional turmoil. Eventually, we will begin to see a shift in our feelings. It may be slight but that doesn't matter. Accept the change willingly and surrender to it. Once we see our loss clearly, without the need to push it away, we are ready to rejoin life and the human race.

Re-engaging with Life

Feeling happy doesn't mean that everything will be perfect all the time: it means we are ready to re-engage and commit to positive action that will gradually improve and enrich our lives. We mustn't feel guilty about positive shifts. Life will still feel hard and there will be many difficult days ahead. Emotions will rise and fall unexpectedly so don't be surprised. Hang on. Accept the experiences as they happen, moment by moment; observe them, let them unfold, good and bad, then return to the breath and surrender.

At first, the full extent of what we have lost is often not entirely understood. A death can throw up other surprising, unexpected and associated losses that we couldn't possibly foresee: the loss of a family unit; the loss of friends; the loss of purpose; the loss of stability; the loss of home; the loss of dreams and expectations; the loss of independence; the loss of confidence and status; the loss of health; the loss of role; the loss of image; the loss of faith; the loss of intimacy.

We mustn't feel guilty about positive shifts.

By accepting the death of somebody central to our lives, we not only have to adjust and cope with a life in which the deceased is forever absent, we have to reconstruct new meaning and discover a different way of being — find a new voice. We have to reassess our own sense of self. We may be required to shoulder roles we find difficult and develop new skills. Although we didn't choose this bereavement, we have to face the challenges it throws our way. Eventually, we may find ourselves pleasantly surprised by newfound proficiencies. This can be very gratifying; a real boost to our confidence.

Death can seem cruel and unfair, making us feel powerless, resentful and helpless. It can leave us feeling guilty that we didn't show enough love or do more while we could – but guilt won't change what has happened or help us face the requirements of our new situation. Acceptance, when it comes, is a sign that we are at last achieving a degree of emotional detachment and objectivity towards our loss, and adjusting to it. When acceptance arrives, however subtle, we will recognize the change. The insane ape is peaceful.

Looking to the Future

Acceptance doesn't equate to a period of happiness or the end of sadness, just the beginning of another trek – a journey on which our loved one accompanies us, but only in our hearts and minds. We will never forget the person who has died – how they looked, their voice or the good times that were shared. We can still celebrate and love them. Why would we ever want to forget somebody who was pivotal and had such an impact on our lives? We can keep their memory alive but we must accept we are now separated and forging a new path.

We must loosen our physical attachment to our departed one and begin looking to the future.

Every twist and turn in this unfamiliar landscape will present challenges and obstacles but somehow we must brave them. We must loosen our physical attachment to our departed one and begin looking to the future. We must never use mindful practice to convince ourselves we no longer feel grief; instead, we must pay attention to where our mind is, moment by moment, and resist clinging on to memories or regretting things that have already happened and are past. The real value of mindfulness lies not simply in the greater appreciation of a blazing sunset but in our greater awareness of our moment-by-moment thoughts and feelings – in building a brighter and more satisfying life.

HEADSTONES & MEMORIALS

The custom of publicly marking our loved ones' graves with poignant tributes, carved granite headstones and bright, floral accolades acknowledges our desire for permanence. We chisel out artistic epitaphs of emotion – memorials – lovingly inscribed with bitter-sweet visions of longing.

GRIEF-STRICKEN, WE WANT TO OWN OUR LOVED ONE; cling on to them forever, preserving their spirit in a life beyond the grave, never allowing them to go. In the face of death we want to stay connected but sometimes, and to our dismay, our words of remembrance aren't the words that others want to hear.

Every relationship is uniquely special and we all have words that capture the essence and meaning of how we feel. The bond we have with our lover, though, is different to that of our lover's connection with their mother. Words can never completely capture the emotional upheaval and pain suffered when a loved one dies but, often, words are all we can offer.

Dust to Dust

Graves, symbols of solid rock, made for the living as well as the dead, become the stone-cold focus for loss, grief and mourning, as well as testaments to social status. They can be the focus of quiet pilgrimage, public displays of emotion, tranquil spots for reflection or, conversely, memorials to regret. They have immense significance to some and little or no importance to others. My parents' ashes are scattered in a spot with no significance – except the memory of our family's grief. On my rare visits I reflect on their continued presence in our lives. A friend's child is buried in a simply marked downland grave; another friend's mother is waiting to be scattered back home in Sri Lanka.

It is important to express what we feel and be true to ourselves but we should be mindful that expressions of love are personal dedications; what is appropriate for one person can appal another. Choosing an inscription, its sentiment, how we verbalize memory, can become a festering sore for family frustration and angry grief – so beware.

When we stand at the grave of a much-loved person, we are paying tribute to their life and the colour they brought to

Memory Boxes

Overcoming grief is not about forgetting the person who has died; it's about finding healthy ways of remembering them and taking them with us on our journey into the future.

We never have to leave our loved ones behind: we can step forwards symbolically, together, hand-in-hand, embracing the new realities of a different life, while holding them lovingly in our hearts and minds. The departed stay with us forever, wrapped in the warmth of our consciousness.

A memory box, physical or digital, is a tribute: a way of celebrating a significant relationship with another human being and coping with their absence. It can be as simple or elaborate as we like; what matters is that the objects placed within resonate with meaning but do not become shrines binding us to the past. Listen to your needs with compassion and an open heart and do whatever feels right for your well-being.

Recollections, happy and sad, are the essence of every important human association. Mementoes of special occasions; letters and photographs; voice recordings; jewellery – personal treasures of a life lived and a relationship held dear. We can open the box and revisit the past occasionally, pay homage and enjoy it, but we can't live there. We have to let it go. Cherish the present; accept the past; face the future and acknowledge the things in life we cannot change.

The pain doesn't last forever,
nothing does — it just feels that way
while we're experiencing it.

ours. Ashes to ashes, dust to dust; we all come from the same source and will eventually return to it. We must learn to love and cherish all the moments in between. We can choose to bury ourselves in the dark with our loved one or we can turn and brave the morning sunlight with hope and courage.

All Things Must Pass
Bereavement is a hinterland, terrifying, a dark void of hopelessness, a landscape without end or boundaries. A journey of loss feels as though it will last forever but as George Harrison sang in 1970, *All things must pass, all things must pass away*, and they do. Mindfulness teaches us that today we are different from yesterday, and from how we will be tomorrow. The pain doesn't last forever, nothing does — it just feels that way while we're experiencing it. The present moment is all we have — NOW — and we must drink every moment deeply. Losing somebody we love feels unbearable but we slowly discover we can bear it. Life will never be as it was but life can still be wonderful. Savour each moment, treasure memories but don't cling on to them. Breathe deeply and turn mindfully towards today.

ANNIVERSARIES & SPECIAL TIMES

Family anniversaries and celebrations, birthdays, significant days such as the date of the bereavement, Christmas and other national festivals can affect us deeply for many years after losing somebody dear to us. Although always poignant, these anniversaries can become, eventually, a commemoration of enduring love.

EVENTS SUCH AS WEDDINGS OR THE BIRTH of a new baby can throw up pangs of sadness and regret when we think about the person who is no longer able to share in our joy. We should embrace these feelings of regret and express them fully in any way that seems natural – even if our reactions may surprise family and friends.

We must guard our emotional health zealously. We must be mindful of how others might be feeling, but never assume we *know*. The way each of us experiences grief is individual, not shared. It is never morbid or melancholic to celebrate a loved one; on the contrary, it can be healthy and therapeutic. Celebrate what was once and is no more – trying not to dwell on the past or cling on to things that are impossible to hold.

We must be mindful of how others might be feeling, but never assume we know.

A Celebration of Happy Times

As time passes, special days can become the focus of happy memories and past times. It might be helpful to plan ahead and decide what to do on those days – to avoid feeling left alone with empty pain. Some of us create traditions such as visiting a grave or place with special associations that remind us of the person who has gone – a pilgrimage. For others, this ritual seems morbid. However hard, we should turn and face the day, building meaning, comfort and healing into it. Often, the anxious anticipation of a forthcoming anniversary can be far worse than the day itself. Be mindful; stay in the present, celebrate the moment.

Do not confuse restoration and recovery with disloyalty. We have to embrace grief in order to recover. But embracing and then letting go of pain is not the same as letting go and forgetting our loved one. Celebration and remembrance of happy times together is true testament to a continuing relationship with the one we love.

Death is nothing at all. It does not count. I have only slipped away into the next room. Nothing has happened. Everything remains exactly as it was. I am I, and you are you, and the old life that we lived so fondly together is untouched, unchanged. Whatever we were to each other, that we are still. Call me by the old familiar name. Speak of me in the easy way which you always used. Put no difference into your tone. Wear no forced air of solemnity or sorrow. Laugh as we always laughed at the little jokes that we enjoyed together. Play, smile, think of me, pray for me. Let my name be ever the household word that it always was. Let it be spoken without an effort, without the ghost of a shadow upon it. Life means all that it ever meant. It is the same as it ever was. There is absolute and unbroken continuity. What is this death but a negligible accident? Why should I be out of mind because I am out of sight? I am but waiting for you, for an interval, somewhere very near, just around the corner. All is well. Nothing is hurt; nothing is lost. One brief moment and all will be as it was before. How we shall laugh at the trouble of parting when we meet again!

CANON HENRY SCOTT HOLLAND
(1847–1918)
✢ *From a sermon preached on 15 May 1910*
in St Paul's Cathedral, London

GEORGE'S STORY

GEORGE was in his early fifties when he sought bereavement help. His father had died three years earlier and his mother, fifteen. He enjoyed very loving relationships with both of them but particularly his mother, Sarah. He was extremely close to her; she had fought a long and loathsome illness bravely, with humour and open-hearted generosity. George and his younger sister, Paula, did all that they could to support their parents practically and emotionally but George lived a considerable distance away and Paula was struggling with her own mental-health problems, which made her unreliable.

When his mum died, George felt his life change irreversibly and her passing sucked all his joy out of living. Her absence, like the sky, spread over everything. His father grieved quietly and then rallied. George visited him regularly and they talked of happier times together when Sarah was alive. He sometimes saw his sister but not always. Life found a new rhythm and then, sadly, his father also died.

George sought help because he knew he was living a harmful and potentially self-destructive life. He was emotionally attuned and worked as a nurse but he had shut down his feelings. He felt frozen. He was drinking heavily, overworking and engaging in risky, unprotected sex with gay strangers that he met online. George had lost so much already. He was afraid of forming deep attachments in case they too died.

George had come out to his parents about his homosexuality in his early twenties and both had been supportive and loving – as he expected. Paula, however, could be abusive and aggressive towards him about his sexuality, especially when she was unwell.

As we talked through his feelings and George unburdened himself, it became clear that he was struggling with suppressed fury towards his sister for what he considered to be her unreliable support of both himself and their dying mother. His anger boiled to the surface in our sessions as he realized why he was so unhappy and why he was so stuck with his grief.

George quickly began making the changes necessary to reach acceptance and forgiveness – to move his life forwards. He started seeing a sex therapist; he cut back his drinking to healthier levels; he changed excessive work patterns and, most importantly, he stopped feeling angry towards his sister.

When his mum died, George felt his life change irreversibly and her passing sucked all his joy out of living.

Summary

George accepted and acknowledged that he and Paula had both done their best to care for their parents. Although his sister had certainly been unreliable, she lived at home so was constantly exposed to her mother's illness. They both did what they could. In accepting this revised reality, George still ached for his mother, but was able to re-engage with his emotions and reignite his joy in living.

JONATHAN'S STORY

JONATHAN was an athletic, handsome young man with a smile that could light up a room, especially when we looked at photographs of his two beautiful children – aged eight and eleven.

His wife Jeanie had died of cancer five years previously and he wept like an injured child when he described their last days together at the hospice. She had battled her tumours bravely but, in the end, nothing could be done and her life had seeped away. Jonathan nursed her with devotion throughout her illness but in the face of the incurable horrors confronting him, he could do little but watch her die. Crucified by nails of grief, and tormented by self-loathing, Jonathan ranted at her death in deep, agonizing cries of pain.

Gradually, an epiphany of self-realization shook him out of his stupor and back into consciousness. He vowed to be both mother and father to his grieving children and rectify his past misdemeanours. He ceased his full-time job as a delivery driver and, with the help of his close-knit family, he learned how to clean, cook and tend to his children.

The house was immaculate; the garden looked glorious; the kids were thriving at school, eating home-cooked food and spending time together; their rooms shone with personality; there were healthy reminders of Jeanie dotted around and the house felt good. Jonathan had also embarked on a new relationship with Sue – a sports trainer whom he met at the children's school and with whom he found joy. The children liked her and Jonathan knew he was falling in love again.

Why then did he keep drawing away from her? Why was he so determined to keep punishing himself with red-hot rods of regret about all the many things that he didn't do? Why couldn't he just accept the wonderful job he was doing with his children? Why wouldn't he recognize they were happy and thriving? Why wouldn't he accept that Jeanie would be proud of him?

Jeanie had been sexually abused as a child. She revealed this early on in their relationship. When they married and started their own family, Jonathan gradually felt pushed away by what he perceived as Jeanie's redirected energy towards the children and her sexual history. Like many, Jonathan buried himself in other women – literally. The affairs weren't important and he covered his tracks well, but just before Jeanie was diagnosed with terminal cancer, the shit hit the fan when she discovered his latest dalliance. As the disease took firm hold and they discussed the future without her, she forgave his misdemeanours and made him promise to fall in love again and be happy.

Jonathan was so swamped by feelings of guilt, remorse and the knowledge of his own selfish behaviour that he couldn't accept forgiveness for past events or a future that promised happiness. He knew Jeanie had forgiven him but he couldn't forgive himself.

Summary

Slowly, Jonathan learned to accept that what had happened could never be altered. He accepted that what mattered now was to reconcile his feelings of regret, feel better about himself and do what he had promised Jeanie he would do – fall in love again, nurture their children, be happy and carry on living.

11. **THE FIRST ANNIVERSARY**

One of the many unhelpful myths about grief is that once we're past the first anniversary, we'll feel better. We'll be over it. Miraculously, something inside our psyches will shift and we'll be flying free, ready to get back out there and re-engage with the fast lane of life.

As the second year approaches, we often find it even harder than the first. The first year is taken up with adjusting and learning to survive; the second, grappling with the harsh reality that our loved one is never coming back. We also have to cope with secondary, often unseen losses that accompany death, such as diminished social networks, loss of status and financial security, loss of faith or sexual intimacy. The roll-call of loss can seem boundless.

Friends and family might express impatience with you for still grieving – but there is no timetable for grief. The only person who knows how you feel is you. Listen to yourself and what you need.

Mindfulness shows us how to accept what is out of our control and commit to action that improves and enriches our lives.

1. By acknowledging your experience, you are acknowledging who you are at this precise moment and developing self-esteem. When practised with tolerance and kindness, you cultivate an attitude of healing compassion towards yourself.

2. Gently redirect your full attention to your breathing. Follow your breath all the way in, then all the way out, counting – inhale one, exhale one, inhale two, exhale two…

3. Allow your attention to expand to your entire body – especially any discomfort, tension or resistance. Say to yourself on your outbreath, 'It's okay; whatever it is, it's okay; let me feel it.'

Allowing unwelcome feelings to simply be there facilitates the realization that we can tolerate the seemingly intolerable.

12. **LETTING GO**

Bereavement is a personal journey, as individual and unique as each life and every relationship. How truthfully we approach the inevitability of death is the difference between experiencing pointless suffering or developing the resilience to rebuild our lives consciously – still cherishing our loved one but turning bravely towards the world again with acceptance and hope.

When somebody significant dies, the physical life with that person is over. Not our love or memories but the shared day-to-day existence with our loved one. When we hold on to someone who has gone, we obscure the very joys, delights and experiences waiting to take us forwards on our journey.

Mindfulness allows us to sink into the very heart of our emotions, seeing what is really there. When we crave an impossible attachment to somebody who is dead, we incapacitate ourselves.

1. Don't try to bear your loss alone; reach out for support to family, friends, support groups and professionals.

2. Have faith in yourself and your own compass of well-being. You know best.

3. Step back from your attachment; try to hold it in a wider perspective, always remembering that even the most unbearable emotions eventually pass.

4. Sit quietly with your grief, reflect, let the waves of sadness wash over you, experience them fully, focus on your breath, try to stay grounded, always bringing yourself back to the present moment and your present experience.

5. Allow things to be as they really are, otherwise you will become trapped and held back by your own needs. Letting go mindfully is the doorway to freedom.

An Afterword

Death has been my companion for sixty years. My father was already fifty when I was born, so my childhood was peppered with funerals. There were no christenings to show the other side of the coin – but, strangely, that did not burden me with a dismal disposition.

Peter Bridgewater and I met at school at the age of sixteen, became good friends, and went on to Farnham Art School together. We have kept in touch through the various births and deaths of our lives but it is only now that we have spoken of our bereavements.

Towards the end of my final school year, my two other closest friends died, and the blues band of which they were the key musicians died with them. Ron Larkin, the lead guitarist, died of a heart attack. He had always had a weak heart, but the other band members never knew. Steve Bruce, the bass guitarist, died in a multiple-collision car accident, along with his father, who was at the wheel.

The love of my life had decided, six months previously, that the future with a world-touring bluesman was too hazardous. It was not the life she wanted. I never became the professional bluesman from whom she parted – but the change came too late. I continued as a solo performer for two years on an ad hoc basis but the British blues boom died. Death, in terms of impermanence as a fact of existence, was an idea with which

I had become familiar from my reading of Buddhism since the age of twelve – and so the integration of this idea into my world view gave me a degree of acceptance lacking in most teenagers. I saw Buddhism in the Shakespeare I studied at school 'We are such stuff as dreams are made on; and our little life is rounded with a sleep.'[31]

I decided I would become an art school lecturer, but that trajectory also died, due to policy changes. So on the successful conclusion of an Illustration degree, my life took another direction: I left for the Himalayas[32] and threw myself into Tantric Buddhism as wholeheartedly as I'd thrown myself into every other fascination in life. The result was immersion in the Nyingma Tradition of Tibetan Buddhism[33] – which emphasizes silent sitting meditation and finding the presence of awareness in the sense fields.[34] Nyingma is the oldest tradition in Tibet. It includes a non-monastic, non-celibate wing[35] which emphasizes everyday life as a method of meditation. Through study and practice as an ordained Nyingma,[36] I came to a radical understanding of life as the alternation of birth and death. Every phase of life is born and dies. The baby I was has died – as has the child and the adolescent. Even adulthood contains many phases. Each day is born and dies – and ultimately the same is true of every moment. I discovered that we have no choice other than to embrace change.

As I looked back over my life I realized that whoever it was, who was looking back, was not the same person. The

Peter Bridgewater I met in my fifties was not the one I knew at art school. I must also have seemed different – and not simply because I had trained as a Lama and experienced three years of solitary retreat in the Himalayas. There would have been similarities but they may have been more misleading than the less obvious differences. My childhood stammer was gone, along with a range of insecurities. My opinions were as strong as ever but I no longer needed to express them with fervency, should they prove unwelcome.

I've written four volumes of memoirs: my 'Portrait of the Artist as a Young Man'.[37] On reading these books, my Buddhist students have commented on the sadness of my life in terms of bereavements and loss. This puzzled me at first because I saw my life as having been happy. This didn't lead to the recognition of denial but to the realization that my life had been characterized by the spacious appreciation in which joy and sorrow are not mutually exclusive. If we cannot appreciate sorrow, the appreciation of joy will be limited by anxiety with regard to the fear of its brevity. Through the spacious appreciation of meditation, we eventually discover that joy and sorrow have one taste that is beyond both joy and sorrow. It is that frame of reference that allows an experience of life that is not conditioned by hope and fear.

Peter's excellent book shows the everyday value of 'mindfulness' – and although this word doesn't figure prominently in the Buddhist lineage I teach, there is an equivalent: *spacious appreciation*.[38] It is obvious that one segues into the other and that spacious appreciation of the sense fields is the key to happiness. That the senses and the sense fields are not separate allows joy and sorrow to dance. I would describe this as the mindfulness of the free mind in the space of the present moment.

In 2013 our son and friend, Robert, died of cancer. Robert was vital, enthusiastic, and humorous. My wife, Khandro Déchen, concurs that the loss of our son is the most painful experience of our lives. Fortunately, as Buddhism is an atheistic religion, we have no one to blame; no sense of fair or unfair; and no cause for anger or depression. There is simply sadness – and the sadness is simple. Our sadness does not preclude the joy of Robert being our son for seventeen years. We have immense appreciation of our time together – and many of these memories still make us laugh. Laughter doesn't preclude tears. We embrace both and cling to neither.

We have no resentment towards the tears or the sensation of sadness. Sadness will not disappear with time – it will simply become part of the texture of spacious appreciation. To some extent that is already the case, as we compile 'The Book of Robert' for his friends. It is impossible to compile such a book without the alternation of grief and pleasure – or to find the mind of the present moment in the one taste of the alternation.

Peter's book will be valuable to those who are bereaved, and to those who are yet to be bereaved. It is good to see him in this new light and to recognize how much we have in common. The cyclic births and deaths of our lives have thus coincided and provided an opportunity: a significant human connection in which two seemingly dissimilar lives arrive at a juncture, where death gives birth to appreciation. Peter has come to understand, through his immersion in 'mindfulness', that anyone can practise spacious appreciation. It is available with or without Buddhism. We are all endowed with senses and we can all learn to be in the moment with those senses.

Spacious appreciation of the passing moment is a catalyst for realizing the nature of our humanity. It reveals life as a fluctuation of joy and sadness,[39] through which spacious appreciation sparkles. Spacious appreciation allows us to discover that the intrinsic awareness of being human is not limited by a rigid identity that demands to be maintained as solid, permanent, separate, continuous, and defined. I was once a bluesman bound for glory. I was once all set to be an art school lecturer. I was a poet – and a series of other individuals, all of whom have died. New individuals will be reborn from what I am now – and they too will die. A stream of memory runs through these many phases of my life, but even the stream of memory changes. It changed with each point in time – and each rememberer. The 'bereaved father of last year' is no longer there – not that I'm no longer bereaved, but because experience changes, becoming increasingly vital: as the texture of appreciation.

Peter asked me '… how it is possible to lose a son without going mad? Did you ever want to scream and rant?' and I replied 'No … I cried … I still cry from time to time – but I have been living with death most of my life; so I have no impulse to fight against reality. Life will never be the same without Robert – but life will never be the same as a result of each day that passes. I shall never forget Robert and shall always miss him – but the senses, in the moment, are simply what they are. In the spacious appreciation of the moment my sorrow is not the solid mass it would be if I identified with it, rather than with the space of the moment.'

We sat with Robert almost continuously in his last days. He was always aware of us, although eventually unable to speak. On his final night of life, we drank a glass of wine together in his room. We toasted, as we always do, with the words *Kèlpa zang* – a Tibetan spiritual drinking toast which means 'we are happy'. *Kèlpa zang*, however, means more than 'happiness' in the conventional sense – it means natural unconditioned happiness, the authentic happiness of spacious appreciation. On hearing our toast, Robert mouthed '*Kèlpa zang*'. These were his last words.

NGAK'CHANG RINPOCHE
✝ *Ngak'chang Chö-ying Gyamtso Ögyen Togden*
✝ *Lama, author & Buddhist teacher*

ENDNOTES

1. *Samaritans* are available 24/7 for anyone experiencing feelings of despair or suicidal thoughts. National helpline: 08457 909090.

2. Extracted from *Grief and The Mindfulness Approach*, (Malcolm Huxter, 1987; see www.buddhanet.net) with additional reference to *Bereavement: Studies of Grief in Adult Life* by Colin Murray Parkes (NY: International Universities, 1987).

3. 'The past is a foreign country: they do things differently there' is the opening line from L.P. Hartley's *The Go-Between*, adapted for the screen by Harold Pinter.

4. Carpe Diem: *Seize the day*. 'While we're talking, envious time is fleeing: seize the day, put no trust in the future.' Horace (Quintus Horatius Flaccus), Roman poet.

5. The analogy of The Buddha helping a bereaved woman deal with the reality of death, from *Grief and The Mindfulness Approach* (Malcolm Huxter, 1987), is further referenced to *The Role of Self-Control Strategies* by Padmal de Silva.

6. My friend Richard Gilpin writes extensively about depression in *Mindfulness for Black Dogs & Blue Days* (Leaping Hare Press, Lewes, UK, 2012).

7. *The Breath (Art of Meditation)* by Vessantara gives clear, helpful instruction and insight into breathing meditations that can transform our lives (Windhorse Publications, Cambridge, UK, 2005).

8. *Mindfulness-Based Cognitive Therapy* (MBCT) was developed by Zindel Segal (Toronto), Mark Williams (Wales) and John Teasdale (Cambridge), based on Jon Kabat-Zinn's *Mindfulness-Based Stress Reduction* programme at the University of Massachusetts.

9. Sarah Silverton gives a detailed account of MBCT in her book *The Mindfulness Breakthrough* (Watkins Publishing Ltd, London, UK, 2012).

10. *Cruse Bereavement Care* offers help and support to the bereaved or those facing death. For more details go to: www.cruse.org.uk.

11. 'Everything is Going to Be All Right' by Derek Mahon, *New Collected Poems* (The Gallery Press, 2011). By kind permission of the author and The Gallery Press, Loughcrew, Oldcastle, County Meath, Ireland.

12. *On Death and Dying* (1969) by Elisabeth Kübler-Ross Swiss American psychiatrist, is now available as a Kindle edition.

13. *Death: The Final Stage of Growth* (1975) by Elisabeth Kübler-Ross is also available as a Kindle edition.

14. There have been numerous attempts at theorising and conceptualising the human response to death. Kübler-Ross (1969) described the process in terms of 'Five Stages of Grief'; Worden (1982) on the other hand argued this might be taken too literally and developed his 'Four Tasks of Mourning' as a way of empowering the mourner to take a more active role in their recovery. For a comprehensive study of bereavement you might refer to *The Many Faces of Bereavement* by Ginny Sprang & John McNeil (Psychology Press, Hove, UK 1995).

15. *Talking with Bereaved People* by Dodie Graves is a user-friendly book that offers wise guidance for talking sensitively to the bereaved (Jessica Kingsley Publishers, London, UK, 2009).

16. Jon Kabat-Zinn began teaching *Mindfulness-Based Stress Reduction* (MBSR) as an eight-week course in 1979, at the University of Massachusetts Medical School.

17. Thich Nhat Hanh's lifelong efforts of generating peace and reconciliation moved Martin Luther King to nominate him for the Nobel Peace Prize in 1967. He lives in south-west France, travelling regularly, leading retreats on happiness and the art of mindful living.

18. Suryacitta Malcolm Smith, aka 'The Happy Buddha', teaches us that happiness is our true nature, our natural state of being, that most of us have lost touch with. *Happiness and How It Happens* (Leaping Hare Press, Lewes, UK, 2011) leads us back towards contentment through mindfulness.

19. *Cruse Bereavement Care* provide free care and bereavement counselling to people suffering the effects of grief.

20. *Death Cafe* is a global movement that helps people become more comfortable with the topic of death. For more information visit deathcafe.com.

21. *Living Well Dying Well* encourages reflection on how to live life fully, while preparing for the end of life. For more information visit livingwelldyingwell.net.

22. *Talking Therapies* are now recognized as an essential tool in the armoury of remedies for treating emotional turmoil, anxiety and depression. If you feel you're not coping, tell your doctor.

23. Commonly found in most households, *paracetamol* (*acetaminophen* in the US) can cause lethal liver damage when taken in excess.

24. My good friend Adam Ford explores the activity of walking as an exercise of body and mind in *The Art of Mindful Walking* (Leaping Hare Press, Lewes, UK, 2012).

25. Zoologist, conservationist and mindfulness author Claire Thompson brings our awareness back to nature in *Mindfulness & the Natural World* (Leaping Hare Press, Lewes, UK, 2013).

26. *Peace is Every Step* by Thich Nhat Hanh (Bantam Books, London, UK, 1991).

27. Stephen Levine explores the whole aspect of physical, psychological, emotional and spiritual healing in *Healing Into Life & Death* (Gateway Books, Bath, 1993).

28. *Samaritans* is a national helpline for people in despair or feeling suicidal. You can call them night or day. For more information go to: www.samaritans.org.

29. *Mind* provides advice and support to anybody experiencing a mental health problem. Visit www.mind.org.uk.

30. *Tales of a Wayside Inn*, Henry Wadsworth Longfellow (1863).

31. *The Tempest*, Shakespeare (Prospero, Act IV, Scene I).

32. *Wisdom Eccentrics* by Ngakpa Chögyam (Aro Books, Inc., New York, USA, 2011).

33. *The Nyingma Tradition* was founded by Padmasambhava and Yeshé Tsogyel – the Tantric Buddhas – in the eighth century.

34. *Spectrum of Ecstasy* by Ngakpa Chögyam and Khandro Déchen (Shambhala Publications, Boston, USA, 2003).

35. The gö kar chang lo'i dé – the white-skirted long-haired lineage.

36. The word *Ngak'chang* – as in *Ngak'chang Rinpoche* – relates to the non-celibate, non-abstemious tantric ordination of the Nyingma Tradition.

37. *An Odd Boy* – four volumes by Doc Togden (Aro Books Worldwide, 2011).

38. Spacious appreciation relates to *the Four Naljors*: shi-nè, lhatong, nyi'mèd, and lhundrüp. Of these practices, 'mindfulness' practice lies within shi-nè and lhatong. Shi-nè is silent sitting in which the mind is emptied of thought. Lhundrüp is the practice of non-discursive observation. These practices are found with the Dzogchen system of the Nyingma Tradition. See *Roaring Silence* by Ngakpa Chögyam and Khandro Déchen (Shambhala Publications, 2002).

39. *Wearing the Body of Visions* by Ngakpa Chögyam and Khandro Déchen (Aro Books inc., 1995).

INDEX

◆

acceptance, meaning of 35
active listening 31–5
afterlife 50, 81, 125
anniversaries 125–6, 132
antidepressants 21, 92, 104–6, 109
atheism 90, 91, 137
awareness 26–7, 117, 121, 135, 138

beginner's mind 35
being present 37
benediction 69
bereavement journals 107
Bhagavad Gita 7
Blake, William 47
blame 60, 61, 71
blessing 69
breath 15, 18–19, 24, 30, 33, 37, 56,
    76, 107, 119, 124, 132, 133
Buddha 16, 61
Buddhism 11, 15, 26–7, 36, 90, 91,
    118, 135–9

child, death of 70–1, 94–5, 111–12,
    115
clearing the house 67–8
compassion 36, 62, 87, 96, 109,
    123, 132
Cruse Bereavement Care 49

Death Cafe 49–50
Death Doulas 50
decision-making 68, 88

eating 57

facing up to death 43–4
faith 84–5, 88, 115
family splits and rifts 63–6
first anniversary 132
five stages of grief 7, 27–30, 44, 45
food 57

forgiveness 25, 47, 64, 73, 75, 87,
    113, 129, 131
four tasks of mourning 44, 45
Freud, Sigmund 73

gardens/gardening 13, 76, 77, 85,
    112
God 60, 83–5, 88, 90, 91
gratitude 101
graves 53, 92–3, 121, 122, 126
Grief Cycle see five stages of grief

Harrison, George 124
headstones 121–2
Holland, Canon Henry Scott 127
hope 27, 34, 101
Horace 144
Huxter, Malcolm 11

Indian burial prayer 23
inheritance 67–9
insane ape 118
intimacy 96
IVF deaths 71

journals 107
Jung, Carl 42

Kabat-Zinn, Jon 34, 35, 36
Kübler-Ross, Elisabeth 6–7, 13, 18,
    27–30, 31, 33, 44, 45, 50
Kumar, Satish 6–7

legacies 67–9
letters to a loved one 51
letting go 26, 35, 47, 127, 133
life after death 50, 81, 125
Living Well Dying Well 50
Longfellow, Henry Wadsworth 117
loving kindness 62–3

madness 11–12, 61, 85, 86, 107
Mahon, Derek 24
Mandela, Nelson 113
meaning 85, 88
medication 21, 92, 104–6, 109
meditation 15, 21, 35, 36, 76, 135,
    136
memorials 121–4
memory boxes 123
Mindfulness-Based Cognitive Therapy
    (MBCT) 21
Mindfulness-Based Stress Reduction
    (MBSR) 36
miscarriage 70–1

natural world 77
Ngak'chang Rinpoche 49, 90, 134–9
non-judging 31, 35, 59, 66
non-striving 35
Nyingma tradition 135

parents, death of 6, 9, 25, 26, 52–3,
    65, 67, 69, 94–5, 128–9
Parkes, Colin Murray 11
patience 33, 35, 107
pets 97
pre-bereavement 45–7

re-engaging with life 118–20, 132
regret 47, 65, 68, 85, 126, 130–1
religion *see* Buddhism; faith; God

Samaritans 39, 59, 103
saying goodbye 46–7
self-destructiveness 63, 118, 128
self-judgement 29, 33, 76, 103, 117
Seven Foundations of Mindfulness
    34–5
sexual intimacy 96
Shakespeare, William 69
siblings 52, 53, 65, 71, 94, 128–9
sleep 56

spacious appreciation 136–8
special times 125–6-
stillbirth 70–1
suicide 6, 9, 25–6, 39, 72–3, 85,
    86–7, 94–5, 102, 108

talking to the dead 51, 54, 93
terminal illness 45–7, 82
Theravadin Buddhism 11
Thich Nhat Hanh 36, 81, 101
Tibetan Buddhism 118, 135
touch 96, 97
transformation 26–7
trust 35, 69, 88, 96

unfinished business 47

walking 76, 77, 84, 97
Worden, J. William 44, 45
writing letters 51

CARPE DIEM: SEIZE THE DAY

While we're talking,
Envious time is fleeing:
seize the day,
put no trust in the future.

HORACE (QUINTUS HORATIUS FLACCUS)
ROMAN POET